··· THE ···
NEW
Cast Iron
SKILLET
& CAST IRON GRIDDLE COOKBOOK

101 Modern Recipes for your Cast Iron Pan
& Cast Iron Cookware

Edition 2

Lisa Brian

HHF Press
San Francisco

Legal Notice

Introduction

In this book, you will learn about the superior cooking benefits of cast iron cookware and discover why professional cooks prefer using cast iron for a variety of food preparation methods. Cast-iron cookware is considered to be among the strongest, most-enduring, best quality products in the marketplace. It consistently earns high marks for cost-effectiveness, durability and excellent results in food quality and presentation. In the chapters that follow, you will discover proven techniques for properly choosing, cooking, maintaining and cleaning cast iron cookware and ensuring its longevity for years to come.

TABLE OF CONTENTS

VEGETABLES AND SIDES 84

Why You Need This Book

Learn How To Sauté, Stir-Fry And Pan-Roast Like A Pro

Cooking with cast iron appliances will undoubtedly enhance the flavor and texture of your food, whether you sauté, stir-fry or pan roast proteins and vegetables. Professionals consistently choose cast iron because of its unique capacity to reach very high temperatures and retain high heat throughout the cooking process.

The ability to maintain this temperature results in perfectly seared, crispy foods. You will discover why this feature is vital to producing delicious foods when utilizing any of these cooking methods.

Learn How To Properly Season Your Pans

Seasoning your cast iron skillet is essential to proper cooking and maintenance. Traditional cast-iron skillets do not have non-stick surfaces. Seasoning entails coating the skillet with cooking oil and baking it in an oven, thereby giving it the shiny, hard surface associated with cast iron skillets. Each subsequent time you heat oil in the skillet, you fortify its nonstick barrier. Seasoning in this manner enables a cast-iron skillet to easily release foods and prevents rusting.

Learn How To Maintain Your Pans So They Last For Generations

One of the biggest misconceptions about cast-iron pans is that they are exceedingly difficult to clean and maintain. You will learn that this notion is far from the truth! In fact, cast-iron pans are highly durable, rarely chip or crack and are a snap to clean. This book will review the best methods for cleaning and storing your pans and you will discover how low-maintenance cast iron can be.

Learn How To Restore Vintage Cast-Iron

Investing in a vintage cast-iron pan has both practical benefits and symbolic appeal. Taking upon yourself to properly restore vintage cast-iron is a labor of love, but it is well worth it! This book will guide you in the restoration process, from tips for purchasing vintage cast iron and detecting flaws, to information on safely stripping old layers of seasoning and removing rust. Once you have removed these layers to expose pure metal, learn how to treat your pan for long term maintenance.

Learn How To Cook Perfectly Prepared Meats, Chicken And Vegetables

Discover how to use cast iron to perfectly sear meats, create browned and crispy chicken dishes and expertly sauté vegetables. The properties of cast iron make it possible to achieve a hard sear on steaks and certain roasts, while also performing like a wok when sautéing vegetable. Your cast iron even doubles as a deep fryer, producing crispy chicken and other fried foods. Get tips inside on proper temperature control, cooking times and food selection for cast iron preparation.

Learn Exciting And Flavorful Recipes For Outdoor And Indoor Cooking

One of the most enticing features of cast iron cookware is its versatility. A cast iron skillet can be used to roast or fry on the stovetop, or alternately pan roast inside a conventional oven. You can use your iron skillet outdoors on a gas or charcoal grill so that various foods can cook simultaneously at different times. Cast iron is ideal for cooking over an open fire, making it the default choice for camping and tailgating events. In this book, you will find delicious, interesting recipes for cooking proteins, vegetables and even breakfast foods both indoors and outdoors with your cast iron skillet.

Family And Friends With An Array Of Expertly Cooked, Versatile Dishes

A cast iron skillet will allow you to cook an entire meal with professional results. Your family and friends will be surprised and delighted with the array of foods you can prepare with a cast iron skillet. From braising a roast to baking sweet or savory cornbread, a cast iron skillet is all you need! Show your friends that delicious food is just as much about the quality of your cookware as the quality of your ingredients.

Choosing the Best Cast Iron Skillet

Evaluating The Quality And Affordability Of Cast Iron Cookware

The top-rated seasoned cast iron pans are both affordable and receive highest praise for their quality and consistency. The Lodge Cast Iron Skillet has regularly earned top marks among other seasoned pans and typically retails for a very affordable price (around $35). Enamel coated skillets require less maintenance but are significantly more expensive, typically retailing for over $150.

Le Creuset has long been the industry leader in enamel cast iron for its durability, lighter construction and wider cooking base.

Seasoned Cast Iron Vs. Enameled Cast Iron

Seasoned cast iron cookware is pre-treated with oil. The major advantage of seasoned cast iron is that it provides non-stick cooking immediately upon initial use. While it is not absolutely necessary to season the pan before first using it, additional seasoning is recommended to achieve the highest quality food in the cooking process. Seasoned skillets often still have tiny porous areas on the surface where metal is exposed.

With prolonged use and washing, the non-stick seasoning may be stripped and requires re-seasoning to maintain its surface. Seasoned cast iron has other advantages, such as providing more uniform heating due its thicker surface as compared to other cast iron cookware. Seasoned cast iron also delivers heat more evenly because of the radiative quality of dark metal.

A second option for cast iron cookware is enamel-surface cookware, which is covered in a layer of enamel (or porcelain) coating and does not require seasoning. Enameled cast iron is therefore easier to clean and maintain.

The enamel coating effectively creates a long-term, durable barrier, and is less prone to rust. Enameled cast iron has the added benefit of being non-reactive, which allows it to hold up to acidic foods unlike seasoned cast iron pans.

Durability of Cast Iron Cookware

Cast iron cookware often survives for generations and remains in excellent condition even after decades of use. Long-time users have claimed that it is nearly impossible to damage a cast iron skillet! One of the main reasons for the longevity of cast iron is that seasoned cast iron is completely resistant to rust. Cast-iron's durability actually improves with continued use and seasoning.

Versatility of Cast Iron Cookware

While cast iron skillets are generally known for their capacity to perfectly sear meat and chicken, these skillets also have a naturally non-stick surface (as opposed to the artificial coating of other non-stick cookware), which allows for superb cooking of omelettes, pancakes and skillet breads. A cast iron skillet can likely replace several old cookware pieces you have in your kitchen; it can be used in place of Teflon pots and pans, roasting pans, deep fryers or even a pizza stone.

Another versatile feature of cast iron cookware is its flexibility in handling various cooking surfaces. You can use it on the stovetop at high heat, place it in the oven at medium to high temperatures or place it directly on top of a grill or coals. These properties make cast iron ideal for everything from quick sautés to recipes that require an initial sear followed by slow cooking in the oven.

Benefits of Cooking with Cast Iron

High Heat Retention

Although cast iron conducts heat slowly, the pan heats fairly uniformly if given sufficient time. Cast iron rarely needs to be placed above a medium heat setting when properly pre-heated. If a high heat setting is necessary, gradually heat the pan and add oil to prevent sticking.

In comparison to a metal like aluminum, a number of hot spots may still form. Nevertheless, the capacity of cast iron cookware to withstand and retain high cooking temperatures make it a popular choice in the cookware market, particularly among seasoned cooks. Once heated, iron consistently holds its heat remarkably well. As such, cast iron is the tool of choice for hot searing - the heat will not escape and food will cook evenly.

Superior Browning Properties

The unique ability to reach and retain high temperatures is what makes cast iron skillets the ideal choice for achieving a well-seared piece of meat. Properly browning, or caramelizing certain foods, seals in its natural juices, and is the key to preparing meat that has deep flavor. Once it reaches a high enough temperature, the intensely hot pan creates a rich, thick crust on the outer layer of meats and burgers, thereby preserving the flavor.

Moreover, searing in a cast iron will create a dark crust without the unwanted burnt bits at the bottom of the pan that typically form during high-heat cooking in non-stick skillets. For similar seasons, cast iron is the vessel of choice for baking cornbread; the uniform-heating and non-stick surface creates a superb browned crust on the sides and bottom of the bread.

Cooking Versatility

~ Stovetop Cooking ~

Stovetop cooking is probably the most popular and common cooking method for cast iron pans due their unique browning capabilities.

Cast iron can be used on a variety of heat sources including gas, electric, induction and ceramic or glass top stoves and ovens. A variety of foods, other than meats, can be cooked on the stovetop using cast iron cookware.

Stovetop cast iron cooking is ideal for omelettes and pancakes, which benefit from the seasoned cast iron pans non-stick surface. Similarly, cast iron functions like a wok, which makes it perfect for all types of stir fried dishes. The key to proper wok cooking is quickly cooking the rice, meats and vegetables to allow the rice to retain a crispy texture, the vegetables to remain crunchy and the protein to cook completely. When using a cast iron skillet, the temperature of the skillet will not decrease upon adding foods to the pan.

~ Oven-Baking ~

A common cooking method for certain cuts of beef requires quickly searing over high heat on the stovetop to develop a browned, flavorful crust, and subsequently cooking it in the oven at a low temperature for an extended time to complete the cooking process.

This technique, known as braising, allows for the use of a single vessel to go from the stovetop to the oven to break down tough tissues in the meat and achieve a tender, flavorful texture.

In addition, the consistent heating and browning properties of cast iron are suitable for various cornbreads, cobblers and other sweet dishes.

~ Grilling/Tailgating/Campfire Cooking ~

Seasoned cast iron cookware is sufficiently heavy and durable to place directly on top of a grill for outdoor cooking. Many manufacturers carry a full line of cookware specifically designed for grilling.

Optimally, cast iron pans and skillets can be used when making dishes on the grill that require different heating times or cooking methods. For example, using cast iron skillet to make fajitas outdoors on a grill is a convenient and popular choice, since the meat can cook directly on the grill top while the sliced vegetables can be stir fried in the skillet. Similarly, it can be used safely on top of an open fire for tailgating and campfire cooking. There are cast iron skillets designed exclusively for camping use.

Large Cooking Surface

The shape and dimensions of a typical cast iron skillet are suitable for cooking large cuts of meat or oversized breakfast or sweet items. The standard skillet has a large cooking surface area and short straight sides. The ample size of the cooking surface ensures maximum contact between the food and the heat.

Increased Dietary Source of Iron

A study by the American Dietetic Association found that cooking in cast iron cookware can leach iron into foods. The foods that are capable of extracting the most iron from a cast iron pan have high moisture contents, are particularly acidic or are cooked for long periods of time. For most individuals and especially for those with an iron deficiency, the addition of small amounts of iron from the cookware is an additional benefit to choosing cast iron.

A History of the Cast Iron Skillet

First Uses Of Cast Iron

Cast iron is essentially iron that is poured into a mold to produce some type of tool. Cast iron pots and pans were originally constructed by making molds from sand and then pouring the molting metal to create the mold's shape.

Prior to the Industrial Revolution, the cooking pots made from cast iron contained three legs or a handle for hanging, as they were intended for use over an open fire. Cast iron cooking in a fireplace was commonplace until cooking tops on stoves were introduced.

Pre and Post Industrial Revolution (1760-1840)

During the late 1700's through the mid 1800's, cast iron cookware was highly valued for its durability and cooking capacity. The cast iron blowing cylinder was invented in 1760, and later improved to accommodate higher furnace temperatures. Subsequent inventions, such as the puddling process for producing a structural grade iron, and hot blasting for preheating air blown into a blast furnace, contributed to more efficient and cheaper ways to produce cast iron for various uses.

Cooking vessels with flat bottoms were created as cooking stoves became ubiquitous during the nineteenth century. Around this time, the flat cast iron skillet was introduced.

The popularity of cast iron vessels is evident in various historical documents and artifacts. Adam Smith wrote in The Wealth of Nations (1776) that a nation's wealth could be surmised from its production of pots and pans. Similarly, in their famous expedition to the Louisiana territory in the early 19th century, Lewis and Clark noted that their cast iron dutch oven was among their most significant possessions. In the 18th and 19th centuries, it was not uncommon for individuals to bequeath their dutch ovens in their wills.

Late 1880's to Mid- 20th Century

In the latter part of the 1800's and the beginning of the twentieth century, cast iron cookware was prevalent in American households. The cast iron vessels of this period, manufactured by the now defunct companies, Griswold and Wagner Ware, are now regarded as highly sought after antiques. Enamel cast iron cookware was also introduced during the twentieth century and became instantly popular.

Prior to the development of Teflon-coated aluminum cookware in the 1960s and 1970s, cast iron remained the overwhelming choice of Americans.

How to Use Your Cast Iron Skillet

Seasoning Your Pre-Seasoned Skillet

Cast iron cookware consistently receives high ratings for quality, durability and affordability. Purchasing a cast iron skillet is a relatively inexpensive, long-term investment for your kitchen, but it does require following specific care and maintenance instructions.

The most important step in ensuring the durability and optimal cooking capabilities of a cast iron skillet is seasoning the skillet. After purchasing your new cast iron skillet, preheat the oven to 350 degrees. Some recommend setting the oven to a higher temperature (around 400-425 degrees) to really seal the coating on your skillet. Wash the skillet with warm, soapy water and a sponge. Do not be afraid to use soap – it will not damage your skillet. Dry the skillet thoroughly after washing.

Apply a thin coating of vegetable oil to the entire surface of the skillet (both inside, outside and the handle) with a cloth or paper towel. Vegetable oil or melted shortening are generally recommended for the seasoning process, but most manufacturers state in their materials that any type of oil can be used. Other popular choices are ghee, flax seed oil or coconut oil.

Once thoroughly coated, place the skillet in the oven upside down on the center rack. Place a pan or sheet of aluminum foil on the bottom rack to prevent oil from dripping to the lower part of the oven. Leave the skillet in the oven for approximately one hour. After one hour, turn off the oven and allow the skillet to cool completely before removing it.

After it has been seasoned, the skillet appears smooth and shiny with a non-stick surface. Cast-iron should be seasoned periodically, particularly any time it exhibits signs of rust or the surface dulls. When food begins to stick to the pan, it is an indication that your skillet should be re-seasoned. Pre-seasoned skillets need to be seasoned as well in order to achieve an ideal non-stick surface. With repeated use of the skillet, food will be less likely to stick to any part of the surface.

Cleaning Your Skillet

While cast iron cookware must be cleaned properly, it is fairly low-maintenance. Once you have finished cooking in your cast iron cookware, rinse it in hot water and scrub the pan surface with a plastic brush. You can adequately clean your pan without using dish soap, but some cast iron cookware users insist on cleaning their skillets with soap. According to manufacturers, while not necessarily recommended, soap does not damage their products.

Soap can generally be safely used because of the molecular changes brought about by the seasoning process. Seasoning creates a thin layer of polymerized oil, which is the result of fat molecules converging to form new, larger molecules. These new molecules build the hard, glossy surface that is characteristic of cast iron cookware. Once the oil has diffused in this manner, the chemicals in dish soap should not alter its properties.

After scrubbing, washing and drying your skillet, season it immediately. Once the skillet is washed and dried, check to make sure there is no longer any moisture in the skillet. Re-season the skillet by again spreading a thin layer of oil over the surface and let dry on the stove over very low heat for several minutes.

Handling And Storing Your Skillet

When handling a cast iron skillet after it has been on the stovetop or in the oven, be sure to wear thick, heavy-duty gloves. The handle of your skillet will get screeching hot!

Storing seasoned cast iron skillets is relatively simple. First, be sure that the skillet is wiped clean and sufficiently cool before storing it. So long as there is no excess oil, you can stack cast iron skillets in any cupboard or pantry. Many cast iron users recommend reducing metal-on-metal contact by placing a paper towel between skillets or pans when nesting them.

A small amount of air circulation is also beneficial particularly in high moisture environments. For this reason, it is preferable not to store skillets and pans with their lids affixed. Alternatively, you can simply leave your cast iron pan on the stovetop until its next use.

Pro-Tips

Heating Cast Iron Cookware Evenly

Cast iron cookware is not known for producing even heating. When you place a cast iron skillet over a high flame burner, you generally get clear hot spots right above the flame, while the perimeter of the skillet remains substantially cooler. In fact, its capacity to transfer heat from one part of the surface to another is significantly weaker than that of other popular cookware materials, such as aluminum.

To remedy its uneven heating properties, place the skillet over a burner and allow it to preheat for 10-15 minutes, while rotating the skillet periodically.

Another method for ensuring consistent temperature in your skillet is placing it in a preheated oven for 20-30 minutes prior to use. Once the pan is sufficiently heated, it will continue to stay hot due to its high volumetric heat capacity. This ability to retain heat will allow you to get a perfect sear on your steak.

Best Way To Restore Damaged And Vintage Pans

Vintage cast iron pans appeal to many enthusiast on several levels. Not only do you get an opportunity to own an impressive historical piece, but vintage cast iron also has some practical advantages. It tends to be lighter than the currently manufactured pans and has a highly smooth finish, which is the result of an old finishing production step that has since been abandoned. You can purchase a cast iron skillet that has already been refurbished or do it yourself.

Selecting vintage cookware. When you have identified a vintage cast iron pan, the first step is to check for flaws. Immediately search for potential cracks in the pan. As some cracks will not be visible under layers of seasoning, experts recommend knocking on the bottom of the pan with your knuckles. A crack-free pan will ring like a bell; a cracked pan will resonate with a blunt, clipped sound. Next, search the pan for pitting. It is best to avoid cookware with excessive number of grooves or uneven texture as achieving an even layer of seasoning is difficult when there is extensive pitting. Some minimal pitting is considered acceptable.

In addition, a pan may show evidence of a reddish color. This usually is not rust, but rather heat damage to the metal. Heat damage cannot be remediated, and these pieces should not be purchased.

Seasoning vintage cookware. The two keys to restoring vintage cookware are eliminating old layers of seasoning and removing rust.

The recommended product for removing old seasoning is lye. A product like Easy-Off is lye based and can be used for cast iron. Spray it on the cookware and seal it in large, durable garbage bags for 24 hours. Lye must be handled carefully to avoid serious chemical burns on the skin. Wearing heavy-duty gloves, an eye mask and protective clothing is highly recommended. After 24 hours, scrub the pans with a heavy duty scrubber. This will remove the seasoning and you will begin to see the original surface, which is gunmetal gray. Using a lye based foam may require several applications until the seasoning is fully removed.

Rust removal for vintage cookware. After the seasoning has been stripped, the next step is to remove rust using white vinegar. Soak the pan in a tub of vinegar for 6-12 hours and then scrub it well. Once the old seasoning and rust have been removed, the exposed metal will begin to rust unless a thin coating of oil is applied immediately.

Using Metal Instruments With Cast Iron Cookware

Many people mistakenly believe that you cannot use metal utensils with cast iron cookware because the seasoning will get damaged and subsequently flake or peel. In fact, however, the seasoning in a cast iron pan is robust and largely resistant to damage from metal utensils. The seasoning is chemically bonded to the metal which makes it unlikely to chip. Many cast iron users prefer metal utensils for cast iron cookware because repeated use of metal utensils will dislodge food residue without disturbing the underlying seasoning. However, only wood, silicone or nylon utensils should be used with enamel cast iron, as metal will most certainly damage the enamel coating.

Oil Skillets Periodically

Cast iron should always be oiled after washing and drying your pan. Regularly applying oil to your pan allows the seasoning to build and prevents rusting.

Foods To Avoid Using In Your Skillet

Certain foods are not ideal for cast iron skillet use. These include very delicate foods, such as flaky fish, especially in a relatively new skillet. Many users prefer cast iron to Teflon for frying or scrambling eggs, but you must have a very well-seasoned skillet to prevent eggs from sticking to the skillet and avoid a messy clean up.

Highly acidic foods, such as tomato based sauces, may interact with any exposed metal and cause damage to a cast iron pan. Similarly, any ingredient with a high acidity level, such as vinegar, wine or citrus, should not be added to a cast iron pan. Besides causing damage to the pan's surface, these   Ingredients may produce a metallic taste when they come into contact with metal. Water, as well, should not be boiled in a cast iron pan or pot as it causes rust to form.

Salt Scrubbing Between Uses

Many cast iron skillet owners routinely use kosher salt and a paper towel to clean their cookware. Particularly when food remnants in the pan are hard to remove, rub the pan with kosher salt and a kitchen towel while the pan is still warm. Once these last food particles are dislodged, coat the pan with oil and it is ready for additional use.

Alternatively, place a spoonful of salt in the skillet with a spoonful of oil. Rub the paste with a paper towel over the skillet in a circular motion. Thoroughly wipe off the salt/oil mixture and re-season the skillet. An added benefit to salting your pan is that the salt contains anti-bacterial properties for cleaning your skillet.

Using Water To Test Pan Temperature

To test the temperature of the skillet, sprinkle several drops of water into the skillet and see if the drops "dance" across the skillet. This is especially important when cooking with cast iron since it takes some time for cast iron to heat to the desired temperature. Foods should not be placed into the skillet until the appropriate temperature is reached.

Products That Should Not Be Used When Restoring Vintage Skillets

There are several products available for restoring vintage cast iron. The best method (as described in Section VII, Pro Tips) is using a lye-based foam such as Easy Off or a lye solution from a hardware store for cleaning large volumes of cast iron. Some sources recommend using Naval Jelly, a form of phosphoric acid, but this should generally be avoided. Once the Naval Jelly is applied it can be very difficult to remove, thereby disrupting the seasoning process. In addition, sandblasting should be avoided as it permanently damages the surface properties of the skillet.

Avoiding Scouring Pads And Long Soaks

When cleaning a cast iron skillet, avoid metal scouring pads to remove stubborn remaining food. These will scratch the surface and remove layers of seasoning. Soaking cast iron in water will have similar damaging effects. Whether one uses soap or simply scrubs the skillet with hot water and a sponge, cast iron should not be left in the sink full of water for an extended period of time.

Consider Purchasing Two Skillets

One of the greatest advantages of cast iron cookery is its versatility – it is just as efficient for searing a steak as it is for baking a sweet cornbread or cobbler. Keep in mind that cast iron skillets tend to capture the flavor of whatever food has just been cooked. Therefore, it is a wise investment to purchase two skillets- one for savory recipes and one for sweet recipes- to avoid comingling the flavors of your steaks and pancakes. Simply wiping down the pan and re-seasoning it will not eliminate the lingering flavor of your prior meal.

How to Store Leftover Food

Do Not Store Your Skillet In The Refrigerator

Leftover food should never remain in a cast iron skillet in the refrigerator. Interactions between the metal of your skillet and the food can cause damage to your cookware and alter the flavors of your food.

~ Food-Metal Reaction ~

Food that is stored in a cast iron skillet in the refrigerator may react with iron and produce an unpleasant metallic taste. The color of the food may even be altered from prolonged contact. It is always preferable to allow food to cool and transfer it to a plastic storage container and the follow the steps for cleaning and seasoning your cast iron skillet.

~ Rust ~

Storing a cast iron skillet inside the refrigerator might cause the skillet to rust as a result of remaining moisture in the food. Removing the rust will disturb the seasoning and require the pan to be seasoned again.

~ Poor Skillet Maintenance ~

When food remains in the pan, acids from the food corrode the seasoning on the skillet's cooking surface. Remaining acid can cause pitting, which alters the non-stick surface of the skillet.

~ Dried Food and Odors ~

Food that remains in a cast iron skillet in a refrigerator may also dry out or develop unpleasant odors. Many cast iron skillets do not contain lids which are useful for protecting the food from excessive drying. In addition, food in cast iron cookware without a lid may pick up odors from other items in the refrigerator or emit odors into the refrigerator.

~Refrigerator Temperature ~

While placing hot foods in the refrigerator is generally not recommended, this is especially relevant with respect to cast iron. Because a cast iron skillet retains heat so efficiently, a hot pan can potentially crack the glass shelves. Moreover, hot food can raise the internal temperature of the refrigerator, and cast iron's capacity for high heat retention can raise the temperature in the refrigerator to dangerous levels.

~ Freezer Storage Not Recommended ~

After food has been cooked in your cast iron skillet, it should be cooled, removed from the cookware and stored so you can immediately clean and season your pan. As discussed above, food that remains in a cast iron pan in a refrigerator will likely have an unpleasant taste and appearance, and the skillet may incur damage. Similarly, storing food in a seasoned cast iron in a freezer is not recommended.

Newer enamel cast iron pans advertise that their cookware is freezer safe. However, sudden shifts in temperature may damage cookware products. Thus, if you remove food in your enameled cast iron from the freezer and place it directly in heat, the drastic temperature shift may cause cracking in the surface.

How to Use This Book

When reading this book, be sure to familiarize yourself first with the usage techniques for cast iron cookware before heading to the recipes section. Learning how to maintain your cookware, both before and after cooking, will enhance your experience with cast iron and ensure the quality and flavor of the recipes you use.

If you don't yet own a cast iron skillet and are considering purchasing one, start with Chapter III to learn about the differences between cast iron and enameled cast iron, and the characteristics of each type of skillet. Once you have purchased a skillet, read Chapter VI (How to Use Your Cast Iron Skillet) to discover how to season, clean and store your cast iron skillet from its first use to maintain its non-stick surface and avoid rusting.

Review the chapter on Pro-tips (Chapter VII) to get useful information about heating your skillet, using utensils, choosing the ideal foods to prepare in cast iron cookware (as well as the foods to avoid), and the preferred ways to clean cast iron. Simultaneously, in Chapter IV, you will learn about the numerous benefits of using cast iron to prepare seared steaks and braised meats, fried chicken, crisp vegetables and perfectly baked items. To ensure you are storing your food safely, review the information in Chapter VIII about the dangers of allowing leftover food to remain in cast iron cookware.

Once you are familiar with how to handle, cook and care for your cast iron cookware, you are ready to scan the recipe section for instructions on preparing sweet and savory foods using a variety of techniques for both indoor and outdoor cooking.

Cast Iron Skillet Book Recipes

In this section, you will discover recipes for delicious foods that can be roasted, baked, fried and sauteed with a cast iron skillet. Preparing foods in cast iron cookware is essential to creating unique flavor, texture and presentation. The recipes are divided into four categories based on type of food:

Protein, Vegetables and Sides, Sweets and Dessert, Breakfast foods.

Within each category you will find recipes that are conducive to stovetop cooking, oven-baking, outdoor grilling or all the above. Be sure to consult Chapters IV and V ("How to Use Your Cast Iron Skillet" and "Pro-Tips") for information on preparing your cookware prior to following the recipes.

Protein

"The table is a meeting place, a gathering ground, the source of sustenance and nourishment, festivity, safety, and satisfaction. A person cooking is a person giving: Even the simplest food is a gift."

Laurie Colwin

Apricot-Tamari Glazed Pan-Seared Chicken Thighs with Cipollini Onions

These chicken thighs are tender and flavorful. The tamari balances the sweetness of the apricot and the citrus imparts a bright note. Chicken thighs work best if you are cooking the dish a day ahead. Cipollini onions are small, thin skinned onions that are perfect for roasting and caramelizing. They naturally have a higher sugar level than yellow or white onions, which is further enhanced by the roasting process.

Yield: 4 servings | Cooking Time: 20 minutes
Nutritional Info: Calories: 588, Sodium: 435 mg, Dietary Fiber: 2.9 g, Total Fat: 22.6 g, Total Carbs: 45.3 g, Protein: 52.0 g.

Ingredients:

2 tablespoons olive oil
4 (6 ounce) boneless, skinless chicken thighs, visible fat trimmed
Coarse salt and black pepper
5-6 cipollini onions, skins peeled
1 tablespoon butter
½ cup apricot preserves
3 teaspoons tamari
1 orange, zested
2 tablespoons lime juice

Instructions:

1. Heat a cast iron skillet over medium heat. Season chicken thighs with salt and pepper. Add the olive oil and chicken thighs. Sear until golden, about 6 minutes per side and transfer to a plate. Add onions and sear until browned and softened. Remove to a plate.

2. Reduce heat on skillet and add butter. Once the butter has melted and starts to foam, add apricot preserves, tamari, zest of orange and lime juice. Add salt and pepper to taste. Stir frequently until sauce reduces, about 8 minutes.

3. Return chicken and onions to skillet and spoon sauce over chicken.

Asian Salmon Burgers with Spicy Mayo Sauce

While white, flaky fish is not recommended for cast iron cooking, more substantial cuts of fish, such as salmon or fish burgers, are ideal. The burgers in this recipe have an Asian flavor, which pairs well with salmon. The center remains moist while the edges do not burn as they might when cooked on top of a grill.

Yield: 4-6 servings | Prep Time: 5 minutes | Cooking Time: 10 minutes
Nutritional Info: Calories: 362, Sodium: 536 mg, Dietary Fiber: 0.6 g, Total Fat: 23.3 g, Total Carbs: 14.2 g, Protein: 24.4 g.

Ingredients For Sauce:

½ cup mayonnaise
2 tablespoons Sriracha sauce
1 ½ teaspoons lime juice
1 teaspoon soy sauce

Ingredients For Salmon Burgers:

2 tablespoons oil
2 tablespoons hoisin sauce
1 ½ pounds fresh or frozen salmon fillet, finely diced
1 tablespoon soy sauce
1/3 cup thinly sliced scallions
2 teaspoons ginger root, finely grated
¾ cup panko crumbs
2 teaspoons lime juice
1 egg, lightly beaten
1 teaspoon toasted sesame oil

Instructions:

1. Mix together sauce   Ingredients. Set aside.
2. Preheat a cast iron skillet over medium-high heat. In a large bowl, gently combine salmon, scallions, panko crumbs, egg, hoisin sauce, soy sauce, ginger, lime juice and sesame oil. Divide the mixture into 4-5 portions and shape the salmon into patties.
3. Add 2 tablespoons oil to skillet. When oil is hot, add patties to the skillet and cook until brown on each side and salmon is cooked through, about 3-4 minutes per side. Remove from skillet and serve on bun with spicy mayo sauce.

Asian Sesame Chicken and Broccoli

This recipe is a great way to have authentic Chinese flavor at home without all the unhealthy additives you normally find in Chinese takeout. Chop broccoli into small sized florets to ensure they cook before they get too brown. Add white rice for a complete meal.

Yield: 4-6 servings | Prep Time: 15 minutes | Cooking Time: 30 minutes
Nutritional Info: Calories: 411, Sodium: 555 mg, Dietary Fiber: 1.1 g, Total Fat: 20.5 g, Total Carbs: 8.7 g, Protein: 46.1 g.

Ingredients:

2 pounds boneless, skinless chicken breasts, diced
Salt and pepper
3 tablespoons flour
1 head broccoli, rinsed, tough stems cut, chopped into small florets
2 tablespoons sesame oil
1 tablespoon olive oil
2 garlic cloves, minced
2 tablespoons tamari
1 tablespoon brown sugar
1 tablespoon mirin
1 tablespoon rice wine vinegar
1 small piece of ginger, minced

48

½ cup chicken stock
3 tablespoon toasted sesame seeds
3 scallions, sliced

Instructions:

1. Preheat oven to 400 degrees.
2. Heat cast iron skillet over medium heat. Combine flour, salt and pepper. Toss with chicken until pieces are coated.
3. Add 1 tablespoon sesame oil, olive oil and chicken to the skillet. Cook chicken until golden on all sides, about 3 minutes per side. Transfer to a plate.
4. Add 1 tablespoon sesame oil into skillet along with broccoli. Sauté until broccoli is browned and softened. Transfer to plate with chicken.
5. Mix garlic, tamari, brown sugar, mirin, vinegar, ginger and stock in a bowl. Pour sauce in skillet and turn heat to low. Add back chicken and broccoli and toss to combine. Place skillet in oven and cook for 20 to 25 minutes. Remove from oven and top with sesame seeds and sliced scallions

BBQ Beef Brisket

Once you have mastered the technique of braising, it is virtually foolproof and always a crowd pleaser. Brisket is a naturally tough piece of meat that requires a significantly long cooking time. The longer you cook it, the softer the meat will become. When purchasing brisket, make sure butcher leaves a ½ inch layer of fat intact. This will keep the brisket from becoming dry.

Yield: 6-8 servings | Prep Time: 15 minutes | Cooking Time: 4 hours and 30 minutes
Nutritional Info: Calories: 87, Sodium: 920 mg, Dietary Fiber: 3.7 g, Total Fat: 2.5 g, Total Carbs: 14.8 g, Protein: 2.9 g.

Ingredients:

1 tablespoon olive oil

Coarse salt and black pepper
4 pound brisket cut
1 tablespoon chili powder
1 tablespoon paprika
1 teaspoon garlic powder
10 medium onions, cut into thick rings
1 ½ cups beef broth
1 cup chili sauce

Instructions:

1. Preheat the oven to 300 degrees.
2. Preheat a cast iron Dutch oven on medium heat. Dry meat and pour olive oil into pot. Combine salt, pepper, chili powder, paprika and garlic powder and pat meat on all sides with spice mixture.
3. Place meat in Dutch oven and sear the brisket. This should take about 8-10 minutes. Make sure you get a thick, browned crust on all sides of the meat. Remove brisket from pot and add onions. Sauté onions, loosening up bits from bottom. Pour in beef broth and stir. Place meat back in pot and cover with lid. Place in oven for 3 hours. After 3 hours, remove and pour chili sauce on top and continue to bake, covered, for another hour or until meat is fork tender.
4. Transfer brisket to a cutting board and let rest. Bring remaining liquid in pot to a boil. Adjust seasonings in liquid. Slice brisket against the grain and pour sauce on top.

Blackened Tuna Steaks

When "blackening" any type of food, a heavy, very hot skillet is required. This preparation generates a considerable amount of smoke; a strong kitchen range hood with decent ventilation is a necessity. Alternatively, prepare this recipe on the grill outdoors. Serve alongside a cool cucumber salad or slaw to cut through the intensity of the blackening seasoning.

Yield: 6-8 servings | Prep Time: 3 minutes | Cooking Time: 10 minutes
Nutritional Info: Calories: 83, Sodium: 40 mg, Dietary Fiber: 0 g, Total Fat: 5.3 g, Total Carbs: 0.0 g, Protein: 8.5 g.

Ingredients:

2 tablespoons canola oil
4 (8-ounce) tuna steaks, preferably sushi-grade
¼ - ½ cup blackening spice

Instructions:

1. First prepare the blackening spice by combining the following: ½ cup freshly ground black pepper, 2 tablespoons kosher salt, 1 tablespoon cardamom, 1 tablespoon ground cinnamon, 1 tablespoon nutmeg, 1 tablespoon ground cloves, 1 teaspoon coriander, 1 teaspoon cumin, 1 teaspoon cayenne pepper and ½ teaspoon celery salt.

2. Preheat cast iron skillet. Place oil inside skillet and wait until smoking. Sprinkle blackening mixture on top of both sides of tuna steaks (about 1-2 tablespoons of blackening spice, depending on how spicy you want your steaks). Add tuna to skillet and cook about 3 minutes each side. The tuna should be browned on the outside and rare on the inside.

Braised Beef in Wine Sauce

When a recipe calls for slow, long cooking, searing the meat first is necessary to caramelize the beef and ensure optimal flavor. Do not skip this step! When preparing this recipe, an enameled Dutch oven works best. Make sure your Dutch oven or casserole dish has a lid, as it will require covered oven-baking after stovetop cooking. High heat should not be used in an enameled Dutch oven as it may cause the surface to crack.

Yield: 6-10 servings | Prep Time: 15 minutes | Cooking Time: 3 hours and 30 minutes
Nutritional Info: Calories: 958, Sodium: 184 mg, Dietary Fiber: 2.1 g, Total Fat: 68.3 g, Total Carbs: 12.8 g, Protein: 60.6 g.

Ingredients:

2 tablespoons butter
2 tablespoons olive oil
5 pound beef chuck roast
Coarse salt and freshly ground pepper
2 Vidalia onions, cut into 1/8ths
4 cloves garlic, minced
4 carrots, quartered
2 medium potatoes, quartered
2 cup good quality dry red wine
1 bouquet garni, containing
2 sprigs thyme, 1 bay leaf,
I bunch parsley,
1 sprig oregano, tied with a string

Instructions:

1. Preheat the oven to 300 degrees. Preheat an enameled cast iron casserole pan or Dutch oven over medium heat.

2. Melt butter and olive oil. Dry meat thoroughly and sprinkle generously with salt and pepper. Place meat in pan and sear until brown on each side, about 4 minutes. Press down lightly with a rubber spatula. Transfer meat to a dish.

3. Add onions, garlic, carrots and potatoes and stir vegetables, scraping up brown bits from bottom until softened, 6-8 minutes. Pour in wine. Add bouquet garni and additional salt. Turn up heat to medium-high and cook for 10-15 minutes until liquid reduces. Place meat inside Dutch oven and cover tightly. Place in oven and cook for 3 hours or longer until meat is very tender. Check meat periodically to ensure that the liquid has not evaporated.

Braised Chicken Thighs with Lemon and Olives

Chicken thighs are perfect for braising; they will not dry out like white meat often does and tend to have more flavor. This one-pot meal incorporates lemons, olives and herbs for a delicious Mediterranean dish that allows you get dinner on the table in no time.

Yield: 2-3 servings | Prep Time: 20 minutes | Cooking Time: 45 minutes
Nutritional Info: Calories: 956, Sodium: 741 mg, Dietary Fiber: 1.4 g, Total Fat: 68.7 g, Total Carbs: 6.2 g, Protein: 67.8 g.

Ingredients:

2 ½ pounds bone-in, skin-on chicken thighs
Coarse salt and black pepper
2 tablespoons olive oil
½ cup dry white wine
½ cup chicken stock, low sodium
4 garlic cloves, minced
5 shallots, sliced
½ cup green olives
3 thyme sprigs
3 rosemary sprigs
1 lemon, juiced (additional lemon slices for garnish)

Instructions:

1. Preheat oven to 400 degrees. Heat cast-iron enameled casserole dish over medium heat.
2. Season chicken thighs with salt and pepper. Pour oil in pan and add thighs, skin side down. Sear until nicely browned, about 4-5 minutes. Flip chicken and cook an additional 3 minutes. Set aside chicken in a dish.
3. Pour in wine and chicken stock and allow to simmer for 10 minutes over medium heat. Meanwhile, scrape up browned bits from bottom of the pan. Add garlic, shallots, olives, herbs and lemon juice. Bring to a boil. Return chicken to pot.
4. Transfer dish to oven until chicken is cooked through, about 20-25 minutes.

Brined Pork Chops

Brining pork chops is a great way to add flavor and ensure that the chop stays juicy throughout the cooking process. Brining both changes the composition of the meat and seasons it. You will not worry about a bland pork chop again! Brining can take a minimum of 30 minutes and up to about 4 hours.

Yield: 3 servings | Prep Time: 45 minutes | Cooking Time: 20 minutes
Nutritional Info: Calories: 326, Sodium: 5824 mg, Dietary Fiber: 0 g, Total Fat: 19.9 g, Total Carbs: 18.3 g, Protein: 18.3 g.

Ingredients:

3 cups cold water, divided
3 tablespoons coarse salt
¼ cup sugar
3 smashed garlic cloves
1 teaspoon black peppercorns
3 pork chops
Olive oil
Coarse salt and black pepper

Instructions:

1. Preheat oven to 350 degrees.
2. Bring 1 cup of water to a boil. Add salt, sugar, garlic and peppercorns and stir to dissolve salt and sugar. Add 2 remaining cups of water to lower temperature of the brine.
3. Place pork chops in a dish and pour brine over chops to cover. Cover with plastic wrap and refrigerate for a minimum of 30 minutes.
4. Preheat skillet over medium heat. Dry chops and coat with olive oil. Sprinkle with salt and pepper.
5. Place pork chops in the hot skillet and sear until golden, about 3 minutes on each side. After browning on both sides, transfer pan to the oven until cooked through. The internal temperature should reach 140-145 degrees.

6. Remove chops from oven and let rest for 10-15 minutes.

Buttermilk Fried Chicken

Not only will a cast iron skillet make your roasting pans obsolete, but you will also be able to ditch the deep fryer. This chicken recipe is marinated in buttermilk and assorted spices. It is important to maintain the heat during the frying process; when the oil temperature lowers, the oil gets absorbed into the chicken and results in overly greasy chicken.

Yield: 3-4 servings | Prep Time: 4 hours | Cooking Time: 45 minutes
Nutritional Info: Calories: 868, Sodium: 293 mg, Dietary Fiber: 1.9 g, Total Fat: 14.5 g, Total Carbs: 38.2 g, Protein: 136.9 g.

Ingredients:

1 whole chicken (around 4 pounds), cut into pieces
½ carton buttermilk
Salt
½ teaspoon cayenne pepper
1 ½ cups flour
½ tablespoon of each of the following: paprika, cumin, garlic powder, onion powder and celery salt
Peanut oil for frying

Instructions:

1. Combine buttermilk, salt and cayenne pepper in a bowl. Several hours before frying chicken, marinate chicken in the buttermilk mixture in the refrigerator. Make sure chicken is evenly coated.

2. Remove chicken from refrigerator and allow to reach room temperature. Combine flour with seasonings.

3. Heat a cast iron skillet. Pour peanut oil in skillet until it comes up to about 1/3 of the skillet. With an instant read thermometer, the temperature of the oil should be about 350 degrees before frying the chicken.

4. Remove the pieces of chicken from buttermilk mixture and shake dry. Dredge in flour. Repeat with remaining pieces. Once oil is hot enough, carefully place chicken in skillet. Keep an eye on the chicken and flip intermittently, making sure it does not burn. The thermometer inserted in the chicken should read about 165 degrees when chicken is fully cooked through.

5. Remove to a drying rack and liberally salt.

Cajun Style Chicken, Mushrooms and Onions

When you need to get dinner on the table in a pinch and have to use what you have in the pantry, this is your meal! The Cajun spices nicely season the chicken and you can add whatever other vegetables you have on hand. This recipe works equally well with boneless, skinless chicken breasts or thighs, or bone-in chicken breasts.

Yield: 3-4 servings | Prep Time: 15 minutes | Cooking Time: 35 minutes
Nutritional Info: Calories: 86, Sodium: 28 mg, Dietary Fiber: 1.4 g, Total Fat: 7.1 g, Total Carbs: 5.7 g, Protein: 1.2 g.

Ingredients:

4 skin-on bone-in chicken breasts or thighs
2-3 teaspoons Cajun seasoning
2-3 tablespoons olive oil
2 Vidalia onions, sliced
1 package button mushrooms, sliced
Coarse salt
½ teaspoon black pepper
6 tablespoons chicken stock

Instructions:

1. Preheat the skillet over medium heat. Preheat the oven to 350 degrees.
2. Sprinkle Cajun seasoning on chicken pieces.
3. Add olive oil to skillet. When skillet is hot, add onions and sauté for a few minutes until they are brown and caramelized. Add mushrooms and sprinkle salt, pepper and a little of the Cajun seasoning on the mushrooms. Sauté until mushrooms are browned and softened. Transfer to a plate.
4. Add chicken pieces and sear for several minutes, depending on the size of your pieces. Add back vegetables and several tablespoons chicken stock to create a sauce. Turn flame to low and cover skillet. Simmer for a few minutes. Place skillet in oven until chicken is cooked through, about 20-30 minutes.

Cheesy Chicken Nachos

This is the perfect snack for your next football party. Load all the toppings inside and serve it to a hungry crowd right from the skillet. If you prefer a dish resembling more of a beef taco, substitute ground beef for the chicken. Serve along with a toppings bar so your guest can customize nachos to their liking.

Yield: 4-6 servings |Prep Time: 15 minutes | Cooking Time: 15 minutes
Nutritional Info: Calories: 668, Sodium: 1314 mg, Dietary Fiber: 4.1 g, Total Fat: 40.3 g, Total Carbs: 45.6 g, Protein: 31.4 g.

Ingredients:

3 tablespoons canola oil
2 cloves garlic, crushed
1 medium onion, diced
2 large chicken breasts, cooked and shredded
½ teaspoon salt
¼ teaspoon pepper
¼ teaspoon paprika

½ cup medium heat salsa
1 cup crushed tomatoes
1 teaspoon taco seasoning
12 ounce package tortilla chips
10 ounces shredded cheese, yellow cheddar and Monterey Jack
For toppings bar: diced red onion, pico de gallo, sliced avocado, sour cream, extra cheese, chopped tomatoes

Instructions:

1. Preheat oven to 400 degrees.
2. Heat a cast iron skillet over medium heat. Add oil, garlic and onion and sauté until onion softens. Add in shredded chicken and sprinkle with salt, pepper and paprika. Pour in salsa, crushed tomatoes and taco seasoning and stir altogether until chicken is coated. Transfer to a plate.
3. Arrange tortilla chips inside skillet. Top with chicken mixture and then with cheese blend. Bake in the oven for 10-15 minutes or until cheese is bubbly. Add your favorite toppings.

Crispy Fried Cod Fillets

While thin fillets are not ideal for a cast iron skillet, firm white fish most definitely are. Purchase thick pieces of cod and the non-stick surface of your skillet will do its job. Serve alongside "Seasoned Beer Battered Onion Rings," which can be found in this book.

Yield: 4 servings | Prep Time: 5 minutes | Cooking Time: 10 minutes
Nutritional Info: Calories: 128, Sodium: 88 mg, Dietary Fiber: 0.8 g, Total Fat: 2.7 g, Total Carbs: 13.9 g, Protein: 12.0 g.

Ingredients:

1 large egg
½ cup milk
1 ½ teaspoons Dijon mustard

4 (6 ounce) cod fillets
1/3 cup all-purpose flour
1/3 cup panko crumbs
Coarse salt
Black pepper
1 teaspoon paprika
½ teaspoon garlic powder
¼ teaspoon cayenne pepper
Vegetable oil
Store-bought tartar sauce and lemon wedges

Instructions:

1. Preheat cast iron skillet over medium heat. Add oil to cover surface.
2. Whisk together egg, milk and mustard. Add cod and remove excess liquid when transferring to flour mixture.
3. Combine flour, panko, salt, pepper, paprika, garlic powder and cayenne pepper. Dredge cod pieces in flour mixture.
4. Place filets in hot pan and cook for 2 to 4 minutes per side, until fish is golden brown on both sides. Transfer to a plate with a slotted spoon and sprinkle with extra salt and pepper. Serve with tartar sauce and lemon wedges.

Crispy Salmon with Lemon-Butter Sauce

Cooking salmon with the skin on allows the fish to cook through and stay moist. Salmon is one of the most nutritious fish you can eat, as it is loaded with omega 3 fatty acids. When possible, choose wild salmon over farmed salmon. Farmed salmon have a different diet and environment, which make them far inferior in terms of nutrition and health profile.

Yield: 4 servings | Prep Time: 15 minutes | Cooking Time: 5 minutes
Nutritional Info: Calories: 220, Sodium: 86 mg, Dietary Fiber: 0.7 g, Total Fat: 18.4 g, Total Carbs: 3.2 g, Protein: 8.9 g.

Ingredients:

4 (4-6 ounce) salmon fillets, patted dry
Salt and pepper
2 tablespoons olive oil
1 large garlic clove, minced
1/3 cup dry white wine
2 tablespoons fresh lemon juice
1 lemon zested
3 tablespoon unsalted butter, diced
2 tablespoons chopped fresh dill

Instructions:

1. Preheat a cast iron skillet over medium heat. Sprinkle salt and pepper on salmon fillets and add 1 tablespoon oil to the pan. To char flesh side, add salmon flesh side down and cook 3-4 minutes. Flip the salmon and cook an additional 3 minutes on skin side. Transfer to a plate.

2. Wipe out skillet and add remaining tablespoon olive oil over medium heat. Add garlic and sauté for 1 minute. Pour in white wine and lemon juice. Stir for one minute. Add lemon zest and continue stirring until slightly reduced.

3. Reduce heat to low and add cubed butter, stirring after each addition. Sprinkle in fresh dill and stir altogether. Season with salt and pepper and pour sauce over salmon fillets.

Dry-Rubbed Flat Iron Steak

This cut of meat is called flat iron because of its shape- an arrow point at one end and a rectangular flat side on the other. Once you coat the steak in the dry rub, it is a good idea to let it sit at room temperature to allow the flavors to meld. For a slightly spicier version, add ¼ teaspoon cayenne pepper to the rub.

Yield: 4 servings | Prep Time: 5 minutes | Cooking Time: 16 minutes

Nutritional Info: Calories: 69, Sodium: 482 mg, Dietary Fiber: 0 g, Total Fat: 7.2 g, Total Carbs: 1.7 g, Protein: 0.4 g.

Ingredients:

1 teaspoon coarse salt
1 teaspoon paprika
1 teaspoon cumin
1 teaspoon garlic powder
1 teaspoon onion powder
½ teaspoon coriander
½ teaspoon thyme
¼ teaspoon black pepper
4 (6 ounce) flat iron steaks
2 tablespoons olive oil

Instructions:

1. Combine salt, paprika, cumin, garlic and onion powders, coriander, thyme and black pepper in a small bowl.
2. Rub the seasonings onto the steaks and drizzle with 2 tablespoons olive oil.
3. Heat a cast iron skillet over medium heat. Place steaks in skillet and sear for 3 minutes on each side. Cook for an additional 3 minutes for medium rare.
4. Let meat rest for 10 minutes before slicing.

Dry-Rubbed Pork Chops

A simple dry rub is often all you need when searing good quality cuts of meat or poultry. This recipe guarantees a moist, flavorful, crisp pork chop and requires very little time to prepare. Bone-on pork chops may take longer to cook, but are more likely to produce a tender chop.

Yield: 4 servings | Prep Time: 15 minutes | Cooking Time: 30 minutes

Nutritional Info: Calories: 172, Sodium: 341 mg, Dietary Fiber: 0 g, Total Fat: 7.2 g, Total Carbs: 0.5 g, Protein: 26.1 g.

Ingredients:

4 bone-on, center cut pork chops
1 teaspoon olive oil
½ teaspoon cumin
½ teaspoon coriander
¼ teaspoon brown sugar
½ teaspoon black pepper
½ teaspoon salt

Instructions:

1. Preheat skillet over medium heat. Preheat oven to 400 degrees.
2. Rub pork chops with olive oil. Combine remainder of spices and sprinkle on chops.
3. Place pork chops in the hot skillet and sear until golden, about 3 minutes on each side. After browning on both sides, transfer pan to the oven until cooked through. Use an instant read thermometer to make sure the internal temperature has reached 140-145 degrees. Start checking the chops after they have been in the oven for 5 minutes, and then check every minute thereafter. This should take no more than 10 minutes.
4. Remove chops from oven and let rest 10-15 minutes.

Flank Steak Fajitas

These fajitas are perfect for cooking outdoors. While the meat cooks on the grill, you can prepare the vegetables in a skillet right on top of the grill. You can even make the tortillas right inside the cast iron pan; see the section "Vegetables and Sides" for the recipe.

Yield: 2-4 servings | Prep Time: 2 hours | Cooking Time: 20 minutes

Nutritional Info: Calories: 452, Sodium: 1900 mg, Dietary Fiber: 4.4 g, Total Fat: 12.6 g, Total Carbs: 52.1 g, Protein: 35.0 g.

Ingredients:

1 pound flank or skirt steak
3 cloves garlic
½ cup soy sauce
½ cup honey
3 sprigs rosemary
Salt and pepper
2 limes, juiced
3 bell peppers of various colors, washed, seeded and sliced
2 medium onions, peeled and sliced into rings
1 box Portobello mushrooms, washed and sliced
Flour tortillas

Instructions:

1. Combine garlic, soy sauce, honey, rosemary, salt, pepper and lime juice in a Ziploc bag. Add steak and marinade for 1-2 hours in the refrigerator.

2. Remove meat from marinade and wipe off excess liquid. Place the cast iron skillet on the grill and heat until smoking. At this point, you can sear the meat in the skillet or directly on the grill. If you cook meat directly on the grill, sear for 3-4 minutes on each side.

3. While meat cooks on the grill, add 1 tablespoon oil to the skillet and place peppers, onions, mushrooms, salt and pepper in the skillet. Allow vegetables to sear. Stir frequently for about 6 minutes. Meat and vegetables should be ready about the same time. Transfer both to a platter and place tortillas in skillet to toast, about 30 seconds. Allow meat to rest. Slice against the grain and serve along with vegetables, salsa and guacamole, if desired.

Greek Style Burger

This Mediterranean twist on the classic burger has a salty, sharp meaty flavor. When combining beef with other   Ingredients, always handle the meat gently or you will end up with an unpleasant texture. Remember the cardinal rule of burger making: do not overmix!

Yield: 8-10 servings | Prep Time: 5 minutes | Cooking Time: 7 minutes
Nutritional Info: Calories: 62, Sodium: 342 mg, Dietary Fiber: 0 g, Total Fat: 4.1 g, Total Carbs: 1.0 g, Protein: 5.0 g.

Ingredients:

1 ½ pounds ground sirloin or chuck
2 teaspoons Worcestershire sauce
½ teaspoon dried oregano
½ cup crumbled feta cheese
1/3 cup finely diced red onion
1 teaspoon kosher salt
½ teaspoon black pepper
Toppings: arugula, sliced tomatoes, store-bought tzatziki sauce

Instructions:

1. Preheat the cast iron skillet over medium heat. While the skillet gets hot, combine beef, Worcestershire sauce, oregano, feta cheese, onion, salt and pepper in a large bowl. Form into 4-5 patties.

2. Place a small amount of vegetable oil in the cast iron skillet. Add burgers to skillet and lightly push down with a heavy duty spatula to ensure contact with pan. Cook about 2-3 minutes. Flip burgers and cook another 2-3 minutes, or until desired doneness. Place burgers in buns and top with tzatziki sauce, arugula and sliced tomatoes.

Hearty Shepherd's Pie

This classic meat-potato meal is filling and hearty. Ground beef is a budget-friendly option when you need to feed a large family. You can adjust seasonings and   Ingredients to suit your preference. After browning ground beef when preparing a one skillet meal, it is always a good idea to drain the excess fat so that it does not accumulate in your dish.

Yield: 8-10 servings | Prep Time: 20 minutes | Cooking Time: 45 minutes
Nutritional Info: Calories: 306, Sodium: 138 mg, Dietary Fiber: 3.9 g, Total Fat: 13.4 g, Total Carbs: 22.2 g, Protein: 24.2 g.

Ingredients:

2 pounds potatoes, scrubbed, peeled and cut into chunks
4 tablespoons butter
¼ cup milk
2 scallions, diced
3 tablespoons of oil
1 large onion, chopped
3 cloves garlic, minced
1 cup each: frozen corn kernels, frozen peas, frozen sliced carrots
1 teaspoon fresh herbs, minced (thyme, rosemary, marjoram)
1 ½ pounds ground beef
2 teaspoons tomato paste
½ cup beef broth

Instructions:

1. Preheat oven to 400 degrees. Place potatoes in a pot of salted boiling water for about 20 minutes and drain.

2. Meanwhile, add 2 tablespoons of oil to a cast iron skillet over medium heat. Sauté onion until soft and browned. Add garlic, corn, peas, carrots, herbs, salt and pepper. Sauté for several minutes. Remove to a plate.

3. Add 1 tablespoon of oil and the ground beef to the skillet. Brown the beef until pink color no longer remains. Drain excess fat with a sieve. Add vegetables back to pan with the beef, tomato paste and beef broth. Reduce heat and cook uncovered for 10 minutes.

4. While beef is cooking, mash potatoes with butter and milk. Add more milk for a creamier consistency, if desired. Mix in chopped scallions.

5. Spread mashed potatoes on top of ground beef inside skillet. Bake in oven for about 20 minutes, or until potatoes are golden brown.

Mini Skillet Meatballs

These meatballs are a perfect size for serving either over spaghetti or as an appetizer with a toothpick. A tasty meatball does not have many   Ingredients, but it must be handled gently. In this recipe, the breadcrumbs are homemade which lends freshness to the dish.

Yield: 8 servings | Prep Time: 20 minutes | Cooking Time: 30 minutes
Nutritional Info: Calories: 273, Sodium: 190 mg, Dietary Fiber: 0 g, Total Fat: 11.6 g, Total Carbs: 4.9 g, Protein: 35.7 g.

Ingredients:

1 egg, lightly beaten
1 pound ground beef
1 pound ground pork or veal
6 slices stale white bread
½ cup grated onion
3 cloves garlic, mined
½ cup grated parmesan cheese
2 tablespoons fresh minced parsley
1 ½ teaspoons Italian seasoning
Coarse salt
Black pepper
2 tablespoons olive oil
Jar of good quality marinara sauce
Extra grated parmesan cheese

Instructions:

1. Preheat oven to 450 degrees. In a food processor, pulse white bread and use 1 cup of the crumbs for meatball mixture.

66

2. In a bowl, gently combine egg, beef, pork or veal, bread crumbs, grated onion, garlic, cheese, parsley, Italian seasoning, salt and pepper.

3. Form into 40 mini-meatballs. Heat skillet over medium heat with 1 tablespoon olive oil. Brown meatballs in skillet, about 5 minutes each side. Heat remaining tablespoon olive oil and work in batches until all the meatballs are browned. Return meatballs to skillet and transfer to oven for 10 minutes.

4. Spoon sauce over meatballs and sprinkle extra cheese on top. Return to oven for 3-4 minutes to heat sauce.

One-Pan Chicken Enchiladas

Next time you have to feed a crowd of adults and children, try this family favorite. Besides requiring almost no other bowls for preparation, this dish does not need to be transferred to a separate serving platter. Serve right out of the skillet for family style meals and an equally elegant presentation.

Yield: 6-8 servings | Prep Time: 15 minutes | Cooking Time: 1 hour
Nutritional Info: Calories: 1832, Sodium: 2909 mg, Dietary Fiber: 4.6 g, Total Fat: 135.5 g,
Total Carbs: 46.0 g, Protein: 110.4 g.

Ingredients:

1 tablespoon olive oil
1 onion chopped
1 cup frozen corn
3 canned chipotle chiles, seeded and minced
1 (28 ounce) can stewed tomatoes
3 cups cooked and shredded chicken (roasted, poached etc.)
12 corn tortillas
Enchilada sauce (canned)
1 ½ cups combination of shredded pepper jack and cheddar cheeses
Cilantro leaves, chopped scallions, sour cream for garnish

Instructions:

1. Preheat oven to 375 degrees.
2. Heat cast iron skillet over medium heat. Sauté onion in olive oil. Add corn, chiles and stewed tomatoes and stir. Add shredded chicken and coat thoroughly.
3. Place chicken on a plate. Wipe out skillet. Spoon about 1/3 of the enchilada sauce on the bottom of the skillet. Spoon chicken mixture into each of the tortillas. Roll tortillas and place seam side down in the skillet. Repeat until skillet is full. Pour remaining enchilada sauce over tortillas and top with cheese.
4. Bake in oven for about 25 minutes. Top with cilantro, scallions and sour cream.

Pan-Seared Thyme and Pepper Crusted Lamb Chops

When cooking lamb chops in a skillet, there is a tendency for the meat to emit a gamey smell that some find unpleasant. You can reduce the odor by trimming as much fat as possible from the lamb. The less fat that melts in the pan, the less aroma your kitchen will have. Soaking and salting the chops for 30 minutes prior to cooking can also help. Just remember to scrape off the salt prior to preparing the chops for cooking.

Yield: 4-6 servings | Prep Time: 15 minutes | Cooking Time: 30 minutes
Nutritional Info: Calories: 387, Sodium: 706 mg, Dietary Fiber: 0 g, Total Fat: 33.1 g, Total Carbs: 1.6 g, Protein: 19.3 g.

Ingredients:

5 garlic cloves, smashed
1 ½ tablespoons fresh thyme, chopped finely
2 teaspoons coarse salt
1 ½ teaspoons fresh black pepper
3 tablespoons olive oil
Squeeze of lime
4-6 1 ¼ inch thick lamb chops

Instructions:

1. Mix garlic cloves, thyme, salt, pepper, 2 tablespoons olive oil and lime juice in a bowl. Stir to incorporate. Dip lamb chops into oil mixture and coat evenly.
2. Preheat oven to 400 degrees.
3. Heat a cast iron skillet over medium heat along with remaining tablespoon olive oil. Add lamb chops and cook until surface develops a browned crust, about 3 minutes per side. Transfer skillet to oven and continue roasting 8-10 minutes, depending on desired level of doneness.
4. Remove from oven and let rest for 10 minutes before slicing.

Rosemary Roasted Veal Chops

Using the stovetop-oven method works beautifully for thicker veal chops. Some cooks recommend wiping the skillet clean after pan-frying and before roasting in the oven to remove excess butter and oil that may burn in the oven.

Yield: 2 servings | Prep Time: 15 minutes | Cooking Time: 30 minutes
Nutritional Info: Calories: 723, Sodium: 1801 mg, Dietary Fiber: 0 g, Total Fat: 9.3 g, Total Carbs: 4.0 g, Protein: 0.2 g.

Ingredients:

2 veal chops
Coarse salt
Black pepper
2 tablespoons olive oil
4 garlic cloves, minced
2 sprigs rosemary, minced
Lemon wedges

Instructions:

1. Remove veal chops from refrigerator and allow to come to room temperature. Preheat a cast iron skillet over medium heat. Preheat oven to 375 degrees.
2. Sprinkle chops with salt and pepper. Once skillet is hot, add olive oil. Place chops in skillet, making sure not to overcrowd the skillet.
3. Sear on all sides until golden brown, about 3-4 minutes. Remove chop from pan and sprinkle with garlic and rosemary mixture. Place chop in oven and roast for 8-10 minutes, turning once.
4. Remove veal chops and allow to rest for 10 minutes. Serve with lemon on the side.

Pepper Crusted Beef Tenderloin

The quintessential seared steak does not need much more than coarse salt, black pepper and a cast iron skillet. Remember to allow time for meat to come to room temperature; placing cold meat directly from the refrigerator onto the stovetop will lead to unevenly cooked steak.

Prep Time: 45 minutes | Cooking Time: 30 minutes
Nutritional Info: Calories: 145, Sodium: 989 mg, Dietary Fiber: 0.6 g, Total Fat: 9.7 g, Total Carbs: 1.6 g, Protein: 13.2 g.

Ingredients:

1 ½ tablespoons black peppercorns, crushed
2 teaspoons coarse salt
4 (6 ounce) beef tenderloin steaks
1-2 tablespoons olive oil

Instructions:

1. In a shallow bowl, combine salt and pepper. Coat steaks on both sides with seasoning. Let steaks rest for 30-45 minutes, or until they reach room temperature.

2. Preheat the oven to 325 degrees. Heat a cast iron skillet for several minutes and add 1-2 tablespoons of oil.

3. When pan is well coated, add steaks and cook for 4 minutes until browned on the bottom.

4. Flip and cook for about 4 minutes on other side. Transfer the skillet into the oven for 4-5 minutes or until a thermometer reads 120-125 degrees for medium rare.

5. Once you remove the steak, tent it with a piece of foil and let it rest for 10 minutes before slicing.

Seared Steak with Mushroom-Wine Sauce

A steak accompanied by a rich sauce makes this a restaurant quality dinner. Be sure to thoroughly pat the meat dry before placing it in a skillet. Meat that has moisture on it will not sear properly. When you place steak inside a smoking hot skillet, press down softly to ensure even contact with skillet.

Yield: 2 servings | Prep Time: 20 minutes | Cooking Time: 22 minutes
Nutritional Info: Calories: 519, Sodium: 1912mg, Dietary Fiber: 1.1 g, Total Fat: 30.2 g, Total Carbs: 26.9 g, Protein: 21.4 g.

Ingredients for sauce:

4 tablespoons butter
½ cup finely chopped shallots
1 cup sliced Portobello mushrooms
½ teaspoon thyme, finely chopped
1 cup Marsala cooking wine
1 cup low-sodium beef broth

Ingredients for steak:

2 boneless beef steaks, such as strip, rib-eye, flat iron or hanger
Coarse sea salt

Black pepper

Instructions:

1. To make the sauce, melt 2 tablespoons butter over medium heat in a cast iron skillet. Add shallots and cook about 2 minutes. Add mushrooms and thyme and sauté until mushrooms soften and give off some liquid. Slowly add wine and simmer for 4-6 minutes until wine reduces. Pour in broth and heat until boiling. Reduce heat and cook 10-12 minutes longer until sauce is reduced to approximately 1 cup. Place remaining butter in skillet and whisk until melted. Transfer to a bowl.

2. To cook the steak, sprinkle with salt and pepper on both sides. Wipe out cast iron skillet and allow to heat for several minutes until smoking. Place steak in skillet and sear on each side, about 4-6 minutes. Place an instant read thermometer on the side of the meat to check the temperature. Remove from pan and let rest for 5-10 minutes. Pour sauce on top of steak prior to serving.

Skillet Chicken Pot Pie

Nothing says comfort food like chicken pot pie! Use refrigerated pie crusts to speed up cooking time. The best part is there is no need to chill, roll out and shape the dough. Cutting slits into the top crust allows steam to escape and prevents the crust from becoming wet and soggy.

Yield: 8-10 servings | Prep Time: 20 minutes | Cooking Time: 45 minutes
Nutritional Info: Calories: 310, Sodium: 1013 mg, Dietary Fiber: 2.2 g, Total Fat: 17.4 g, Total Carbs: 17.9 g, Protein: 20.4 g.

Ingredients:

1/3 cup butter
4 shallots, sliced
1/3 cup flour
1 ½ cups chicken broth
½ cup half and half

72

1 tablespoon of each of the following: paprika, salt, garlic powder, onion powder and dried oregano
½ tablespoon cayenne pepper
2 tablespoons olive oil
1 package Portobello mushrooms, sliced
1 cup frozen peas
1 cup carrots, thinly sliced
4 cups diced cooked chicken
1 package refrigerated pie crusts
1 egg white

Instructions:

1. Preheat oven to 350 degrees.
2. Heat cast iron skillet over medium heat. Melt butter and stir in shallots. Stir in flour and whisk for 1 minute. Slowly add in chicken broth and half and half and whisk vigorously for 5 minutes. Add all the seasonings and remove skillet from heat. Transfer to a bowl.
3. Heat olive oil in skillet and once hot, add mushrooms. Sauté until mushrooms soften, giving off their liquid. Add peas and carrots and sauté 6-8 minutes. Add diced chicken and give a big stir. Transfer to bowl with sauce. Wipe out skillet.
4. Place 1 pie crust into the greased cast iron skillet. Spoon filling into pie crust and top with remaining pie crust. Brush with egg white and cut a few slits in top crust. Bake for 1 hour or until golden brown.

Skillet Chicken Sausage and Red Beans

If you cannot find sausage in bulk, simply buy the links and remove the casings before browning the meat. Creole seasoning is a mixture of paprika, dried oregano, dried basil, dried thyme, black pepper, cayenne pepper, salt, granulated onion and granulated garlic. You can purchase a pre-made creole spice blend or prepare the seasoning at home and store it for future use.

Yield: 2-4 servings | Cooking Time: 15 minutes
Nutritional Info: Calories: 183, Sodium: 655 mg, Dietary Fiber: 6.4 g, Total Fat: 5.8 g, Total Carbs: 19.8 g, Protein: 13.9 g.

Ingredients:

1 tablespoon olive oil
½ pound spicy chicken sausage
1 onion, sliced thin
3 garlic cloves, minced
1 teaspoon creole seasoning
½ cup chicken or vegetable stock
15 ounce can kidney beans, drained and rinsed
2 tablespoons flat fresh leaf parsley

Instructions:

1. Heat olive oil in cast iron skillet and break up sausage in skillet, sautéing until browned, 3-4 minutes.
2. Add onion and sauté until softened, 4 minutes. Add garlic and seasoning and stir. Add the stock and cover the pan, cooking 2 minutes.
3. Uncover, add the beans and sausage and cook another five minutes. Take skillet off the heat. Sprinkle with parsley.

Seared Scallops and Spinach

When cooking scallops, a blazing hot skillet is necessary for developing that deep, brown crust essential to a well-cooked scallop. This caramelization provides most of the flavor in this simple, healthy meal.

Prep Time: 3 minutes | Cooking Time: 10 minutes
Nutritional Info: Calories: 32, Sodium: 69 mg, Dietary Fiber: 2.0 g, Total Fat: 0.4 g, Total Carbs: 5.8 g, Protein: 2.9 g.

Ingredients:

12 jumbo sea scallops
Olive oil
Kosher salt
Freshly ground black pepper
3 shallots, diced
6 garlic cloves, sliced
12 ounces fresh baby spinach
½ lemon juiced

Instructions:

1. Heat skillet over medium-high heat. Use paper towels to pat scallops dry.
2. Sprinkle scallops with salt and pepper. Add oil to the pan. Once oil is smoking, place scallops in the pan and cook 2-3 minutes on each side.
3. Reduce heat to medium and add oil to pan.
4. Place onion and garlic in the pan and sauté until onions are nicely browned. Add spinach in batches until wilted.
5. Sprinkle with salt and pepper.
6. Remove from heat and sprinkle with fresh lemon juice.
7. Place spinach on platter with scallops on top and serve.

Skirt Steak with Chimichurri Sauce

This recipe works equally well with flank steak. Always slice this cut of meat thinly and against the grain to avoid chewy, tough pieces. The chimichurri sauce can be used as a marinade, or drizzled on top of the steak and served on the side as a dipping sauce. The Argentine variety, as presented below, does not contain cilantro, as other variations do.

Yield: 4 servings | Prep Time: 2 minutes | Cooking Time: 8 minutes
Nutritional Info: Calories: 727, Sodium: 182 mg, Dietary Fiber: 1.5 g, Total Fat: 51.9 g, Total Carbs: 3.0 g, Protein: 61.3 g.

Ingredients:

2 pounds skirt steak
1 tablespoon olive oil
Coarse salt
Black pepper
½ cup extra virgin olive oil
2 tablespoons red wine vinegar
1 jalapeno, seeded and diced
2 cloves garlic, minced
Sea salt
Black pepper
1 cup flat leaf parsley, chopped
1/8 cup fresh oregano leaves

Instructions:

1. For the chimichurri sauce, combine vinegar, jalapeno, garlic, salt, pepper, parsley and oregano in a food processor and pulse for 1 minute. Slowly drizzle in ½ cup extra virgin olive oil. Set aside. The sauce may be refrigerated for up to 1 week.

2. For the steak, preheat a cast iron skillet over medium high heat. Season the skirt steak with salt and pepper. Pour in 1 tablespoon olive oil once skillet is smoking. Sear for 2 to 3 minutes on each side. Let rest before slicing.

Spicy Panko Crusted Seared Salmon

The panko crumbs that coat this salmon are flavored with Dijon mustard and prepared horseradish. It provides a sharp, tangy flavor that complements the richness of the salmon. Sear the salmon on the skin side so as not to burn the panko, and finish off in the oven so crumbs get brown and toasted.

Yield: 4 servings | Prep Time: 15 minutes | Cooking Time: 15 minutes
Nutritional Info: Calories: 152, Sodium: 70 mg, Dietary Fiber: 0 g, Total Fat: 13.3 g, Total Carbs: 0.8 g, Protein: 8.5 g.

Ingredients:

4 (6 ounce) salmon fillets
3 tablespoons olive oil
1 cup panko crumbs
2 teaspoons prepared horseradish
3 teaspoons Dijon mustard
1 teaspoon prepared minced garlic
Salt and pepper
2 tablespoons chopped parsley

Instructions:

1. Preheat oven to 450 degrees.
2. Preheat cast iron skillet over medium heat.
3. Dry salmon fillets with paper towels.
4. Heat cast iron skillet over medium heat. Add 2 tablespoons olive oil and wait until oil shimmers.
5. Combine panko crumbs, horseradish, mustard, minced garlic, salt, pepper and 1 tablespoon olive oil in a bowl. Add more oil if necessary. Texture of crumbs should be similar to damp sand.
6. Dip salmon on flesh side into the panko mixture and press down crumbs to adhere to fish.
7. Place fish in skillet skin side down and sear 2-3 minutes. Place skillet in hot oven on top rack to toast crumbs and finish cooking fish, about 2-3 minutes, depending on how rare you prefer your salmon.

Steakhouse Rib Eye

The heat retention properties of cast iron produces a browned exterior you normally get only from the high heat appliances of an industrial kitchen at a steakhouse. You can sear this steak in cast iron on the outdoor grill or indoors on your stovetop and then transfer it to the oven.

Yield: 6 servings | Prep Time: 5 minutes | Cooking Time:20 minutes
Nutritional Info: Calories: 369, Sodium: 1376 mg, Dietary Fiber: 0 g, Total Fat: 26.2 g, Total
Carbs: 1.0 g, Protein: 31.0 g.

Ingredients:

2 (1 ½ pound) bone-in rib-eye or porterhouse steaks
Coarse salt and black pepper
1 teaspoon steak seasoning
2 tablespoons vegetable oil
5 tablespoons butter
6 garlic cloves, smashed

Instructions:

1. Sprinkle steaks generously with salt, pepper and steak seasoning.
2. Preheat a cast iron skillet over medium-high heat. Add oil and steak to the skillet. Cook 5-7 minutes, until exterior turns dark and crusty. Flip steak and repeat. If you prefer a medium-rare steak, the temperature should reach between 120-125 degrees. For a more well-done steak, place it in the oven for continued cooking.
3. With skillet on the stovetop, turn down the heat, push steaks to the side and add butter and garlic cloves. Cook 3 minutes or until butter starts to foam. Spoon sauce over steak several times. Transfer steak and butter sauce to platter and let rest before slicing.

Sweet and Sticky Short Ribs

Short ribs are cut either English style (parallel to the bone) or en-style (across the bone). Either will work, but English style are meatier and make for a nicer presentation. As short ribs tend to be fatty, a useful tip for eliminating much of the fat is to place ribs in the refrigerator after cooling and wait several hours. The fat will rise to the top and you will easily be able to skim it off.

Yield: 6 servings | Prep Time: 2 hours and 15 minutes | Cooking Time: 4 hours and 15 minutes
Nutritional Info: Calories: 130, Sodium: 1339 mg, Dietary Fiber: 0 g, Total Fat: 0.1 g, Total
Carbs: 30.9 g, Protein: 1.9 g.

Ingredients:

3 pounds shirt ribs, English cut
½ cup soy sauce
1 cup light brown sugar
¼ cup Thai sweet chili sauce
5 garlic cloves, smashed
Salt and black pepper, to taste
1 inch piece of grated ginger
½ cup beef broth
½ cup water

Instructions:

1. Preheat oven to 300 degrees.
2. Combine soy sauce, brown sugar, sweet chili sauce, garlic, salt, pepper and ginger in a bowl. Place ribs in marinade for 1-2 hours in the refrigerator. Remove ribs and reserve marinade. Pat dry.
3. Heat a cast iron Dutch oven over medium heat. Place ribs in pot but don't crowd the vessel. Sear on all sides, 3-4 minutes per side. Brown the ribs in rotation if necessary. Place all ribs back in pot. Mix the reserved marinade with the water and broth and pour into the Dutch oven. Cover with lid and cook in oven for 3-4 hours, or until meat is falling off the bone.
4. When ribs are done, refrigerate them with the sauce. After fat has been skimmed, you can pour sauce into pot and heat to reduce it slightly.

Tasty Turkey Burgers

Turkey burgers may not be an exact substitute for meat burgers, but you can still achieve a flavorful and juicy patty made of ground turkey. Although oil is optional in many beef based recipes, turkey is naturally lean and needs the additional fat. Ideally you should avoid purchasing very lean ground turkey for this recipe.

Yield: 4 servings | Prep Time: 5 minutes | Cooking Time: 8 minutes
Nutritional Info: Calories: 1239, Sodium: 1024 mg, Dietary Fiber: 0 g, Total Fat: 77.7 g, Total Carbs: 23.1 g, Protein: 127.1 g.

Ingredients:

2 tablespoons oil
1 pound ground turkey
3 tablespoons minced shallots
2 cloves minced garlic
2 tablespoons Worcestershire sauce
1 ½ tablespoons seasoned bread crumbs
1 teaspoon onion powder
½ teaspoon celery salt
¼ teaspoon black pepper
Dash of tabasco sauce

Instructions:

1. Heat a cast iron skillet over medium-high heat. Add the oil to the pan. Meanwhile, combine turkey, shallots, garlic, Worcestershire sauce, bread crumbs, spices and tabasco in a medium sized bowl. Make sure   Ingredients are well distributed. Form the mixture into 4 patties.

2. Add turkey burgers to skillet and lightly push down with a heavy duty spatula. Sear burgers on one side for about 2-3 minutes, or until browned. Flip burgers and cook until browned and cooked through (another 5 minutes or so). Remove burgers from skillet and toast buns in same skillet, if desired.

The "Perfect" Burger

We all have eaten our share of outdoor grilled burgers. But a truly delicious burger -one that has wonderful flavor and texture -must cook in its own fat and not on a grill grate. These burgers are ideally cooked in a cast iron skillet on top of your grill- that way you avoid the hassle of a very smoky kitchen!

Yield: 8-10 servings | Prep Time: 5 minutes | Cooking Time: 5 minutes
Nutritional Info: Calories: 133, Sodium: 360 mg, Dietary Fiber: 0.7 g, Total Fat: 6.8 g, Total Carbs: 9.6 g, Protein: 8.0 g.

Ingredients:

1 ½ pounds ground chuck
1 teaspoon coarse salt
½ teaspoon black pepper
1 white onion, sliced into rings
4 slices cheddar cheese (optional)
4 soft buns (such as potato buns), split

Instructions:

1. Sprinkle ground beef with salt and pepper. Gently form the meat into 4 balls. Press the balls lightly into patties, 4-inches wide, 1-inch thick. Place an indentation in each burger's center with your thumb.

2. Place cast iron skillet on top of your outdoor grill and heat until it starts to smoke. Pour a small amount of vegetable oil into the skillet. Place burgers in skillet and lightly push down with a heavy duty spatula. After about 2-3 minutes, place sliced onion on top of burger. Flip burgers carefully so onions are on bottom and place a slice of cheese on alternate side. Cook 2 more minutes or until cheese melts. Serve burger on toasted bun, if desired.

Veal Piccata

This classic preparation originated in Italy with veal as the main star. Today, in America, it is most often prepared with chicken. When making piccata, the veal or chicken is pounded thin between pieces of wax paper and then shallow fried.

Yield: 4 servings | Prep Time: 5 minutes | Cooking Time: 15 minutes
Nutritional Info: Calories: 324, Sodium: 388 mg, Dietary Fiber: 1.0 g, Total Fat: 24.4 g, Total Carbs: 10.3 g, Protein: 15.0 g.

Ingredients:

4 (6 ounce) veal cutlets
1 lemon, juiced and zested, separately
1/3 cup flour
Salt and Pepper
1-3 tablespoons olive oil
3 tablespoons white wine
3 tablespoons capers
½ cup chicken broth
3 tablespoons unsalted butter
¼ cup fresh chopped parsley

Instructions:

1. Place each piece of veal between waxed paper and pound with a mallet until 3/8 inches thick. Sprinkle with lemon juice. Dredge in flour seasoned with salt and pepper.
2. Heat cast iron skillet over medium heat. Pour 1 tablespoon oil into skillet. Add veal cutlets and sauté for 1-2 minutes each side. Transfer to plate.
3. Pour off any drippings and deglaze pan with white wine. Add capers, broth and lemon zest, scraping up browned bits. Simmer for 5 minutes until sauce reduces.
4. Add butter and parsley to the sauce. Add back chicken and serve in skillet.

Skillet Roasted Chicken

Forget your old tools for roasting a whole chicken- once you roast a chicken in a cast iron skillet, you will never go back to another method. Chicken must be brought to room temperature prior to roasting to ensure even cooking. This method can be outdoors right on top of a grill if indoor roasting creates too much smoke.

Yield: 3-4 servings | Prep Time: 20 minutes | Cooking Time: 1 hour
Nutritional Info: Calories: 640, Sodium: 215 mg, Dietary Fiber: 0.6 g, Total Fat: 24.4 g, Total Carbs: 2.0 g, Protein: 98.8 g.

Ingredients:

1 3 pound chicken
4 tablespoons olive oil
Coarse salt and freshly ground pepper
1 lemon juiced
1 tablespoon assorted herbs, finely minced (such as thyme, rosemary, sage, marjoram or any combination thereof)

Instructions:

1. Preheat oven to 450 degrees. Place your cast iron skillet in oven while oven preheats.

2. Combine oil, salt and pepper, lemon juice and herbs. Pat chicken dry with paper towels. Rub oil mixture all over chicken.

3. Place the seasoned chicken onto the hot skillet in the oven. Chicken should roast between 40-45 minutes. Let chicken rest for 10-15 minutes before slicing.

VEGETABLES AND SIDES

"You don't have to cook fancy or complicated masterpieces - just good food from fresh ingredients."

Julia Child

"Almost Like French Fries" Potatoes and Onions

We all know the best part of a roasted potato is the crisp brown exterior. But when roasting in the oven, sometimes the result is soft and mushy. The key to these potatoes is to let them sear on the skillet without touching them. They need sufficient time to crisp up without being moved around.

Yield: 4 servings | Prep Time: 10 minutes | Cooking Time: 50 minutes
Nutritional Info: Calories: 97, Sodium: 22 mg, Dietary Fiber: 2.2 g, Total Fat: 0.3 g, Total Carbs: 22.6 g, Protein: 2.6 g.

Ingredients:

1 Vidalia onion, sliced
Olive oil, enough to cover bottom of the skillet
Small Yukon gold potatoes, around 1 ½ -2 inches in size
Coarse kosher salt
Fresh ground pepper

Instructions:

1. Heat the cast iron skillet over medium-high heat. Place onions inside skillet and fry for several minutes until browned. Season with salt and pepper. Transfer onions to a bowl.

2. Slice potatoes in quarters. Add enough olive oil to cover the skillet. (Oil should come up 1/8 inches in skillet). Sprinkle a layer of salt into the skillet. Add potatoes to skillet with cut side facing down. Fry about 10-12 minutes without moving or turning potatoes.

3. At about 12 minutes, check if potatoes are properly browned. When potatoes are all seared, cover with a lid and cook about 20 minutes. They will continue to cook through and stay warm until serving.

Buffalo Style Cauliflower

Buffalo style cauliflower is an easy, flavorful side dish or party appetizer. This is another great example of how you can adapt familiar flavors into vegetarian dishes. Cauliflower is firm and substantial when broken into florets and takes on whatever flavors you may add. Serve alongside ranch dressing and celery sticks for dipping.

Yield: 4 servings | Prep Time: 15 minutes | Cooking Time: 25 minutes
Nutritional Info: Calories: 132, Sodium: 442 mg, Dietary Fiber: 1.8 g, Total Fat: 12.9 g, Total Carbs: 4.7 g, Protein: 1.5 g.

Ingredients:

2 tablespoons olive oil
1 head cauliflower
Salt and pepper
2 tablespoons unsalted butter
¼ cup Frank's red hot sauce
1 tablespoon fresh lime juice
Chopped parsley or cilantro

Instructions:

1. Preheat oven to 375 degrees.
2. Prep the cauliflower: Chop off tough flower part at the base of the cauliflower. Break into small to medium sized florets.
3. In a microwave safe bowl, melt butter. Add hot sauce and lime juice to butter and stir.
4. Heat a cast iron skillet to medium-low heat. Add oil and cauliflower florets. Sauté until nicely browned, 4-5 minutes. Pour in hot sauce mixture and stir to coat evenly.
5. Place in oven for 15-20 minutes until cauliflower is softened.
6. Remove from oven and sprinkle with parsley or cilantro for freshness.

Buttermilk Biscuits

Buttermilk biscuits can be served with dinner or breakfast with either jam or butter. This recipe does not require any kneading or rolling. Keep oven rack on the highest position to prevent the bottom of the biscuits from burning.

Yield: 10 servings | Prep Time: 20 minutes | Cooking Time: 15 minutes
Nutritional Info: Calories: 155, Sodium: 158 mg, Dietary Fiber: 0.7 g, Total Fat: 5.1 g, Total Carbs: 23.9 g, Protein: 3.6 g.

Ingredients:

1 cup all-purpose flour
1 cup whole wheat flour
2 tablespoons sugar
4 teaspoons baking powder
¼ teaspoon baking soda
¼ teaspoon salt
4 tablespoons softened butter
1 ¼ cups cold buttermilk

Instructions:

1. Preheat oven to 400 degrees.
2. In a large bowl, combine flours, sugar, baking powder, baking soda and salt. Add softened butter and use your fingers to work the butter into the flour until the mixture resembles coarse crumbs.
3. Stir in the buttermilk, forming a soft dough.
4. Turn the dough onto a floured surface and pat into a ¾ inch thick circle. With a 2 inch biscuit cutter, cut out biscuits, gathering dough as needed to shape more biscuits.
5. Arrange biscuits in skillet and transfer the oven to bake until golden brown, about 12 minutes.

Cheesy Eggplant Parmesan

This eggplant parmesan can be made in one skillet. Dredge eggplant in the breading, fry it, and then simply add the other   Ingredients and bake in the oven. The finished product presents so beautifully that it could be served to company.

Yield: 4-6 servings | Prep Time: 20 minutes | Cooking Time: 30 minutes
Nutritional Info: Calories: 248, Sodium: 573 mg, Dietary Fiber: 4.4 g, Total Fat: 13.3 g, Total Carbs: 22.5 g, Protein: 11.2 g.

Ingredients:

1 large eggplant, sliced
1 egg
Salt and pepper
1 cup seasoned breadcrumbs or panko crumbs
2 tablespoons olive oil
1 cup store bought marinara sauce
1 cup shredded mozzarella cheese
¼ cup parmesan cheese

Instructions:

1. Preheat oven to 400 degrees. Heat cast iron skillet over medium heat. Lightly beat egg with salt and pepper. Dip eggplant slices into egg. Pour breadcrumbs onto plate. Dip eggplant into breadcrumbs.

2. Heat oil in pan. Place breaded eggplant slices in skillet and fry until golden brown. Pour marinara sauce in skillet and top with shredded cheese. Bake in oven for 15 minutes, or until cheese melts Sprinkle with parmesan and sea salt.

Crisp Skillet Roasted Brussel Sprouts

A cast iron skillet does wonders for more than just meat and poultry- once you roast your veggies in a cast iron skillet, you will taste the difference. The intense heat generated by contact with the skillet allows vegetables to crisp up in a way that that surpasses oven roasting. These vegetable-based recipes are endlessly versatile. You can add a variety of herbs or nuts for variety, such as basil, hazelnuts or parmesan cheese.

Yield: 4 servings | Prep Time: 15 minutes | Cooking Time: 20 minutes
Nutritional Info: Calories: 200, Sodium: 29 mg, Dietary Fiber: 4.6 g, Total Fat: 16.7 g, Total Carbs: 12.2 g, Protein: 5.2 g.

Ingredients:

1 pound Brussel sprouts, trimmed, tough outer parts removed
3 cloves garlic, minced
1 teaspoon cider vinegar
3 tablespoons olive oil
Salt and freshly ground pepper
¼ cup pine nuts, toasted

Instructions:

1. Preheat oven to 350 degrees.
2. Heat cast iron skillet over medium heat. Place Brussel sprouts in skillet and they will begin to brown. Add garlic, vinegar, oil and salt and pepper.
3. Place skillet in oven and cook for 20 minutes. Shake skillet periodically to ensure sprouts are not burning and are well coated with oil. Remove from oven and sprinkle with toasted pine nuts.

Crunchy Parmesan and Garlic Zucchini

This side dish balances the creaminess and sweetness of caramelized zucchini with the savory crunch of a panko crumb topping. Some cooks recommend salting zucchini in a colander for 30 minutes prior to cooking to leach out some of the water from this high water-content vegetable.

Yield: 4-6 servings | Prep Time: 15 minutes | Cooking Time: 20 minutes
Nutritional Info: Calories: 135, Sodium: 59 mg, Dietary Fiber: 2.4 g, Total Fat: 8.3 g, Total Carbs: 12.2 g, Protein: 3.6 g.

Ingredients:

3 tablespoons olive oil

4-6 small green zucchini, sliced into spears by cutting into ½ lengthwise and then into
thirds
Coarse salt and pepper
4 garlic cloves, sliced thin
1 cup panko crumbs, seasoned with salt, pepper and paprika
1 cup freshly grated parmesan or Romano cheese

Instructions:

1. Preheat oven to 450 degrees.
2. Heat oil in a large cast iron skillet on medium-low heat.
3. Layer zucchini in skillet. Let brown on one side for 3 minutes and flip over pieces, browning as many spears as you can. Sprinkle with salt and pepper. Add sliced garlic and sauté for 1 minute.
4. Sprinkle panko crumbs and grated cheese on top. Transfer to oven until brown and bubbly, about 5-10 minutes.

Curried Acorn Squash and Rice Dinner

This dish packs a lot of flavor from the addition of curry. You can adjust the heat level depending on the type of curry you use. Curry powders are blends of various spices in different proportions. You can use basic yellow curry or a blend such as Ras El Hanout or Garam Masala. Curry powders are potent spices, so add gradually depending on the type you are using.

Yield: 2-4 servings | Prep Time: 15 minutes | Cooking Time: 1 hour
Nutritional Info: Calories: 338, Sodium: 213 mg, Dietary Fiber: 8.4 g, Total Fat: 13.3 g, Total Carbs: 47.9 g, Protein: 10.1 g.

Ingredients:

1 tablespoon olive oil
1 clove garlic, minced

1 small onion, diced
1 ½ cups acorn squash, peeled and cubed
1-2 tablespoons curry powder
Salt and pepper
½ cup white rice
2 medium tomatoes, chopped
½ cup chickpeas, drained and rinsed
½ cup coconut milk
1 tablespoon tomato paste
1 cup vegetable broth

Instructions:

1. Heat a cast iron skillet over medium heat. Add olive oil, garlic and onion and sauté several minutes. Add squash and sauté 5-6 minutes. Add curry powder, salt, pepper and rice into skillet and stir.

2. Add tomatoes, chickpeas, coconut milk and tomatoes paste to skillet and stir well. Cook until tomatoes start to break apart.

3. Pour in vegetable broth and bring to a boil. Reduce to low and continue to simmer until liquid reduces. Continue cooking until most of the liquid is absorbed by the rice and rice is tender, about 40-45 minutes. Serve in skillet.

Crispy Asian Green Beans

Peanut oil is preferable to olive oil or other oils when cooking at higher temperatures since it has a higher smoke point. For a more elegant presentation, choose French green beans, or haricot verts. Haricot verts are slimmer and have smaller seeds than standard green beans.

Yield: 4 servings | Cooking Time: 5 minutes
Nutritional Info: Calories: 52, Sodium: 7 mg, Dietary Fiber: 3.9 g, Total Fat: 1.9 g, Total Carbs: 8.6 g, Protein: 2.2 g.

Ingredients:

> 1 teaspoon peanut oil
> 1 pound green beans, ends trimmed
> 2 cloves garlics, minced
> Coarse sea salt
> ½ teaspoon toasted sesame oil

Instructions:

1. Heat skillet on medium heat and add peanut oil until it shimmers. Add garlic and cook about 30 seconds. Add green beans and salt to the pan and roast until golden brown. In the last minute of cooking, drizzle on toasted sesame oil.

Garlicky-Lemon Zucchini

When choosing zucchini, skip the really large pieces and choose smaller ones. They have fewer seeds and are more flavorful. Ensure that the pan is hot enough to avoid winding up with squishy, watery pieces. You can add yellow squash to this recipe for more color.

Yield: 2-3 servings | Prep Time: 5 minutes | Cooking Time: 5 minutes
Nutritional Info: Calories: 93, Sodium: 1 mg, Dietary Fiber: 2.8 g, Total Fat: 7.0 g, Total Carbs: 7.0 g, Protein: 1.6 g.

Ingredients:

> 4 small green zucchini, any color, sliced about ¼ inch thick
> 1 ½ tablespoons extra virgin olive oil
> 1 tablespoon garlic, minced
> Coarse salt and black pepper
> ½ teaspoon thyme, minced
> ½ lemon

Instructions:

1. Heat cast iron skillet over medium-low heat. Add oil and let heat for 1 minute.
2. Sprinkle zucchini with salt and pepper. Add to the pan in a single layer. When zucchini is nicely browned, flip and brown on other side. Add garlic and sauté for one minute. Sprinkle thyme and additional salt if necessary.
3. Remove from pan and squeeze lemon juice on zucchini.

Ginger Infused Kabocha Squash

This Taiwanese inspired dish is a nice alternative to butternut squash. Kabocha squash is among the sweeter varieties of squash, similar to a pumpkin or yam. Kabocha squash have a very tough exterior and can be difficult to cut. When possible, purchase kabocha squash pre-cut at the market.

Yield: 4 servings | Prep Time: 15 minutes | Cooking Time: 10 minutes
Nutritional Info: Calories: 82, Sodium: 1 mg, Dietary Fiber: 0 g, Total Fat: 7.1 g, Total Carbs: 4.9 g, Protein: 0.4 g.

Ingredients:

2 tablespoons canola oil
1 piece ginger, peeled and cut into thin strips
Kosher salt and pepper
1-2 teaspoons maple syrup
1 kabocha squash, peeled, seeded and cut into 1 ½ inch pieces

Instructions:

1. Preheat oven to 400 degrees.
2. Heat skillet over medium heat and add oil. Cook ginger in oil until fragrant, 1-2 minutes.

3. Toss squash in a bowl with salt, pepper and maple syrup. Add squash to the skillet and sear for 2 minutes on each side or until browned. Cover skillet and place in oven until squash cooks through.

Glazed Carrots

These carrots develop a wonderful glaze and retain their crunch. The thyme and parsley not only complement the sweetness of the carrots, but add vibrant color to this side dish. Serve alongside heavily seasoned chicken or pork for a nicely balanced meal.

Yield: 4-6 servings | Prep Time 3 minutes | Cooking Time: 10 minutes
Nutritional Info: Calories: 135, Sodium: 59 mg, Dietary Fiber: 2.4 g, Total Fat: 8.3 g, Total Carbs: 12.2 g, Protein: 3.6 g.

Ingredients:

6 medium carrots, peeled and cut into thirds, crosswise, then cut into halves so you have spears
3 tablespoons butter
2 teaspoons honey
Coarse salt and pepper
¼- ½ cup water
½ teaspoon chopped thyme
Bunch flat leaf parsley, chopped

Instructions:

1. Heat cast iron skillet over medium heat. Melt butter and place carrots in skillet, cut side down. Carrots will brown quickly, about 3 minutes.
2. Add honey, salt, pepper, water and thyme and stir everything together. Stir constantly until carrots are cooked and coated with honey, about 4-5 minutes.
3. Sprinkle fresh parsley on top.

Gnocchi with Cherry Tomatoes and Basil

This dish takes just minutes to complete with the help of store bought, pre-prepared gnocchi. Do not overcook tomatoes or they will become too liquidy. This recipe can also be made into a complete meal with the addition of chicken or sausage. The oven to table presentation makes this dish worthy of company.

Yield: 6 servings | Prep Time: 15 minutes | Cooking Time: 15 minutes
Nutritional Info: Calories: 177, Sodium: 484 mg, Dietary Fiber: 2.2 g, Total Fat: 6.5 g, Total Carbs: 25.1 g, Protein: 4.5 g.

Ingredients:

1 pound store-bought gnocchi
2 tablespoons olive oil
2 cloves garlic, minced
1 pint yellow and red cherry tomatoes
Coarse salt and pepper
1 cup fresh basil (loosely packed)
½ cup grated parmesan cheese

Instructions:

1. Preheat oven to 400 degrees.
2. Heat a large pot of salted water and cook gnocchi according to package directions.
3. Heat a cast iron skillet over medium heat. Add olive oil and sauté garlic for 1 minute.
4. Add tomatoes, cooking until blistered, but not saucy. Sprinkle in a good amount of salt and pepper.
5. Stir in gnocchi and sprinkle basil and parmesan on top.
6. Transfer to oven and bake 8-10 minutes until bubbly.

Green Bean Casserole with Crunchy Onion Topping

This is the perfect side dish recipe for your thanksgiving meal! This recipe does way with condensed cream of mushroom soup. It uses fresh mushrooms and cream to create a smooth consistency. Green beans are generally blanched and then submerged in an ice bath to halt the cooking process and maintain their crisp texture.

Yield: 4-6 servings | Prep Time: 15 minutes | Cooking Time: 35 minutes
Nutritional Info: Calories: 247, Sodium: 245 mg, Dietary Fiber: 3.2 g, Total Fat: 17.1 g, Total Carbs: 17.6 g, Protein: 5.3 g.

Ingredients:

1 pound fresh green beans, rinsed and trimmed
2 tablespoons unsalted butter
1 tablespoon olive oil
12 ounces button mushrooms, trimmed and sliced
3 cloves garlic, minced
2 shallots, sliced
Salt and pepper
2 tablespoons all-purpose flour
1 cup chicken broth
½ cup heavy cream
½ cup whole milk
1 ½ cups French fried onions

Instructions:

1. Preheat the oven to 450 degrees.
2. Boil a gallon of salted water in a saucepan and add beans. Boil for 5 minutes. Drain in a colander and plunge into a bowl of ice cold water.
3. Melt butter and olive oil in a cast iron skillet. Add mushrooms and stir until some liquid evaporates. Add garlic and shallots and a generous sprinkling of salt and pepper. Cook for 2 minutes. Sprinkle flour in and mix for 1 to 2 minutes. Add the

broth and turn down the heat to medium-low. Pour in cream and milk and stir for 8-10 minutes until sauce thickens.

4. Stir in the green beans and combine well. Sprinkle fried onions on top to cover. Bake in oven for 20 minutes until onions brown and sauce is bubbly.

Ham Mac n' Cheese

This mac n' cheese gets delicious flavor from the combination of sharp cheeses, the saltiness of the ham, the crunch of the fried onions and the kick of the hot pepper sauce. Any pasta works fine but cavatappi is a hollow shaped corkscrew pasta that has a nice bite and adheres well to the cheese.

Yield: 6 servings | Prep Time: 15 minutes | Cooking Time: 20 minutes
Nutritional Info: Calories: 602, Sodium: 926 mg, Dietary Fiber: 3.6 g, Total Fat: 24.5 g, Total Carbs: 63.9 g, Protein: 28.7 g.

Ingredients:

1 pound cavatappi
¼ pound ham, chopped
2 tablespoons butter
1 ½ cup whole or 1% milk
½ cup chicken or vegetable stock
½ teaspoon paprika
1 teaspoon salt
¼ teaspoon pepper
1 teaspoon hot pepper sauce, or more to taste
2 ½ cups grated gruyere and cheddar cheeses
3 tablespoons all-purpose flour
¾ cup prepared crunchy fried onions

Instructions:

1. Preheat oven to 400 degrees.

2. Bring a pot of salted water to a boil and cook pasta according to package directions. Meanwhile, heat a cast iron skillet over medium heat.

3. Sauté ham in a little olive oil for 3 minutes.

4. Place butter in hot skillet. Pour in milk, stock, paprika, salt, pepper and hot pepper sauce. Whisk together. Add cheese to the skillet, whisking frequently. When it is melted, add flour slowly, whisking constantly to thicken. Add cooked ham.

5. Drain pasta and transfer to the skillet. Top with crunchy onions. Place skillet in oven and bake 10-15 minutes or until browned.

Herbed Focaccia Bread

Many local pizzerias sell their in-house dough so you can purchase fresh, high quality pre-made dough. Serve with marinara or pesto sauce for dipping. Always use heavy duty gloves and a durable pot holder when pulling a hot cast iron skillet out of the oven.

Yield: 6 servings | Prep Time: 15 minutes | Cooking Time: 30 minutes
Nutritional Info: Calories: 118, Sodium: 132 mg, Dietary Fiber: 0 g, Total Fat: 10.8 g, Total Carbs: 2.8 g, Protein: 3.3 g.

Ingredients:

1 package pizza dough, defrosted if necessary
Flour for dusting
3 tablespoons extra virgin olive oil
1 tablespoon prepared minced garlic
2 teaspoons chopped fresh rosemary
Salt and pepper
2 tablespoons grated Romano cheese (optional)

Instructions:

1. Preheat oven to 400 degrees and place skillet inside oven.

2. Roll out pizza dough on floured surface. Stretch out to a 12 inch circle.

3. Remove skillet from oven and coat with 1 tablespoon olive oil. Add dough to skillet and carefully stretch up the sides. Sprinkle with remaining olive oil, garlic, rosemary, salt, pepper and cheese (if desired). Bake until golden brown, about 30 minutes. Slice into wedges.

Indian-Spiced Cauliflower Steaks

Cauliflower steaks are a wonderful vegetarian option when you are craving a more substantial meal. You can use a cast iron skillet to roast this cauliflower like you would any piece of steak. Each head of cauliflower should provide 2-3 steaks.

Yield: 2-4 servings | Prep Time: 15 minutes | Cooking Time: 15 minutes
Nutritional Info: Calories: 336, Sodium: 538 mg, Dietary Fiber: 4.1 g, Total Fat: 1.3 g, Total Carbs: 64.0 g, Protein: 5.3 g.

Ingredients:

I head cauliflower
Olive oil
Salt and pepper
1 teaspoon curry powder
½ teaspoon ginger
¼ teaspoon turmeric
Handful of cilantro leaves, chopped

Instructions:

1. Preheat oven to 350 degrees.
2. Prep the cauliflower: Chop off tough flower part at the base of the cauliflower. Slice vertically into 5 ½- ¾ inch steaks. Don't worry if some florets break off as long as you have most of the piece intact.
3. Place cast iron skillet over medium heat.
4. Add 1-2 tablespoons olive oil. Coat steaks with olive oil and sprinkle with salt, pepper, curry powder, ginger and turmeric. When skillet is smoking, arrange cauliflower steaks inside and cook until charred, 2-3 minutes. Flip over and cook

another minute. This process may have to be done in batches depending on the size of your skillet.

5. Place skillet in oven and roast for 10 minutes. Sprinkle with additional salt and cilantro leaves.

Mexican Brown Rice Bake

This casserole-like dish has all the familiar flavors of Mexican food, but uses fresh and healthy   Ingredients. Try to purchase the quick cooking brown rice as brown rice can take substantially longer to cook than white rice. Don't substitute regular paprika for the smoked variety the recipe calls for; smoked paprika has a distinctive flavor and adds depth to the dish.

Yield: 6 servings | Cooking Time: 30 minutes
Nutritional Info: Calories: 382, Sodium: 310 mg, Dietary Fiber: 2.2 g, Total Fat: 18.2 g, Total Carbs: 31.1 g, Protein: 22.9 g.

Ingredients:

2 tablespoons olive oil
1 Vidalia onion, chopped
1 green pepper and 1 red pepper, chopped
1 jalapeno, seeded and chopped
1 cup diced tomatoes, seeded and chopped
1 cup frozen corn
1 teaspoon cumin
1 teaspoon smoked paprika
½ teaspoon each: sweet paprika, coriander and salt
Pinch red pepper flakes
1 tablespoon tomato paste
1 cup quick cooking brown rice
1 can black beans, rinsed and drained
2 cups vegetable broth
1 cup shredded cheddar cheese

Lime wedges, chopped cilantro and flour tortillas

Instructions:

1. Heat a skillet over medium heat. Add olive oil, onion, peppers, jalapeno, tomatoes, corn, cumin, paprikas, coriander, salt and red pepper flakes.

2. Cook for 10 minutes until vegetables are tender and well coated with spices. Add tomato paste and brown rice and stir constantly. Stir in black beans and vegetable broth. Bring to a boil.

3. Turn down the heat and let simmer, covered for 15 minutes, or until most of the broth is absorbed and rice is tender.

4. Sprinkle with cheddar cheese and allow to melt for a few minutes on stovetop. Remove from heat and squeeze lime juice over rice bake. Sprinkle cilantro on top. Serve with toasted tortillas on the side.

Miso-Maple Roasted Brussel Sprouts

This combination of salty and sweet will truly satisfy your taste buds. Miso is a thick paste made from fermented soybeans. White miso is fermented for a shorter time and has less salt than the darker varieties and is therefore more delicate in flavor than yellow or red miso. Maple syrup complements the distinctive umami flavor.

Yield: 4 servings | Prep Time: 5 minutes | Cooking Time: 25 minutes
Nutritional Info: Calories: 200, Sodium: 672 mg, Dietary Fiber: 5.2 g, Total Fat: 8.5 g, Total Carbs: 28.9 g, Protein: 6.0 g.

Ingredients:

2 tablespoons olive oil
1 pound Brussel sprouts, trimmed, tough outer parts removed, sliced in half
3 cloves garlic, minced
¼ cup white miso
1/8 cup apple cider vinegar

¼ cup maple syrup
¼- ½ cup water

Instructions:

1. Heat cast iron skillet over medium heat. Place olive oil, garlic and Brussel sprouts in skillet. Cook undisturbed until nicely browned, 4-5 minutes.
2. Place in oven and continue cooking about 20 minutes until sprouts soften, shaking skillet occasionally.
3. Mix miso, vinegar, maple syrup and water together. Remove Brussel sprouts from oven and return to stovetop over low heat. Pour in miso mixture and stir until evenly coated. Cook on stovetop over low to medium heat until some of the liquid evaporates and thickens.

Pancetta and Asparagus with Fried Egg

Pancetta and eggs make this recipe a hearty side dish or light lunch. When cooking vegetables in a cast iron skillet, don't set the heat above medium or medium-low. While ideally the vegetables should caramelize, you don't want them to burn before cooking (softening) sufficiently.

Yield: 2-4 servings | Prep Time: 15 minutes | Cooking Time: 10 minutes
Nutritional Info: Calories: 229, Sodium: 687 mg, Dietary Fiber: 1.2 g, Total Fat: 17.6 g, Total Carbs: 3.4 g, Protein: 14.6 g.

Ingredients:

1 tablespoon olive oil
¼ pound pancetta
3 small shallots, sliced thin
½ pound asparagus, tough ends broke off, sliced into 1 inch pieces
Salt and pepper
2 eggs

Instructions:

1. Heat olive oil in a cast iron skillet over medium heat. Fry the pancetta, stirring frequently. Transfer to a plate.

2. Add shallots and cook for 2 minutes. Add asparagus pieces and sauté for several minutes. Sprinkle with salt and pepper and continue to watch closely that asparagus is browned and cooked through. Add pancetta back to the pan and stir together. Transfer to a plate.

3. Add a little oil if necessary and fry an egg in pan. Top asparagus pancetta mixture with fried egg and season with salt and pepper.

Potato Au Gratin Bake

This indulgent potato recipe allows you to first make the sauce and then compose the final product in a single skillet. Leftovers should always be removed and placed in a separate container so as not to damage the pan or alter the taste of the food.

Yield: 6 servings | Prep Time: 15 minutes | Cooking Time: 1 hour and 5 minutes
Nutritional Info: Calories: 355, Sodium: 278 mg, Dietary Fiber: 2.8 g, Total Fat: 18.0 g, Total Carbs: 36.2 g, Protein: 15.1 g.

Ingredients:

3 tablespoons unsalted butter
3 tablespoons flour
½ cup half and half
½ cup of milk
3 cloves minced garlic
1 teaspoon onion powder
Salt and pepper to taste
6 medium Yukon Gold potatoes, peeled and thinly sliced, preferably using a mandolin
1 cup shredded Gruyere cheese
1 cup shredded Fontina cheese
1 bunch parsley, chopped finely

Instructions:

1. Preheat oven to 450 degrees.
2. Heat a cast iron skillet over medium heat. Once hot, melt butter and add in the flour, whisking for 45 seconds. Add half and half, milk, garlic, onion powder, salt and pepper and whisk until smooth and not lumpy. Pour mixture into a separate bowl.
3. Place sliced potatoes in bottom of skillet in an overlapping pattern. Sprinkle both cheeses on top of each layer of potato. Pour milk mixture over potatoes, season with salt and pepper and sprinkle remainder of cheese on top. Cover with foil and bake for 45 minutes to 1 hour. Once potatoes are cooked, remove foil and bake in oven until top layer is golden brown. Remove from oven and sprinkle with parsley.

Scallion Cornbread

There are dozens of differing opinions on how cornbread should be made. Some purists insist there is no sugar in authentic cornbread. This version calls for just one tablespoon but feel free to omit it. Flour helps the cornbread stay together when it is sliced.

Yield: 8-10 servings | Prep Time: 15 minutes | Cooking Time: 35 minutes
Nutritional Info: Calories: 135, Sodium: 225 mg, Dietary Fiber: 2.5, Total Fat: 4.2 g, Total Carbs: 20.8 g, Protein: 3.9 g.

Ingredients:

¾ cup flour
1 cup coarse cornmeal
1 tablespoon sugar
1 ½ teaspoons baking powder
½ teaspoon baking soda
½ teaspoon salt
½ teaspoon pepper
1 cup milk
2 eggs
2 tablespoons unsalted butter

1 bunch scallions, chopped
½ cup frozen corn, thawed

Instructions:

1. Preheat oven to 400 degrees. Whisk together flour, cornmeal, sugar, baking powder, baking soda, salt and pepper. In a separate bowl, whisk together milk and eggs.
2. Heat a cast iron skillet over medium heat. Melt butter in skillet. Sauté scallions and corn for about 3-4 minutes.
3. Whisk milk mixture into flour mixture. Pour inside skillet and stir in scallions and corn.
4. Transfer skillet into oven and bake 20-30 minutes, until toothpick comes out clean.

Seafood and Vegetable Paella

Paella, a rice dish that comes from Valencia, Spain, is traditionally cooked in a Paellera. A large cast iron skillet works just as well. A paella is a wonderful dish because it can be endlessly customized. It can include seafood, chicken or sausage or be made as a vegetarian dish. Have all your   Ingredients prepped and chopped beforehand so that you can add things quickly while the skillet is on the stove.

Yield: 4-6 servings | Prep Time: 5 minutes | Cooking Time: 25 minutes
Nutritional Info: Calories: 382, Sodium: 310 mg, Dietary Fiber: 2.2 g, Total Fat: 18.2 g, Total Carbs: 31.1 g, Protein: 22.9 g.

Ingredients:

1 tablespoon paprika
2 teaspoons extra virgin olive oil
3 boneless, skinless chicken thighs, chopped
6 ounces Mexican chorizo
2 shallots, chopped
Coarse salt and pepper

3 cloves garlic, minced
Flat leaf parsley, chopped
2 vine-ripened tomatoes, chopped
1 tablespoon tomato paste
2 teaspoons smoked paprika
Pinch of red pepper flakes
1 cup long grain white rice
6 ounces large shrimp, peeled, deveined and chopped
1/2 cup frozen peas
Lemon wedges

Instructions:

1. Preheat cast iron skillet over medium heat.
2. Place broth in a pot and simmer over low heat.
3. Sprinkle paprika and onto chicken.
4. Heat olive oil and place chicken in pan. Sear chicken about 5-8 minutes. Transfer to a plate and add chorizo, breaking it up as it cooks, for about 5 minutes. Transfer to chicken plate.
5. Add shallots, salt and pepper, garlic and parsley and sauté until onion softens. Add tomatoes, tomato paste, smoked paprika and red pepper flakes. Sauté until tomatoes start to release their juices.
6. Add rice and hot broth to skillet and stir to combine with tomato mixture. Transfer chicken and chorizo into skillet, cover and simmer until rice absorbs the broth, about 15 minutes. Add shrimp and peas and cover again for another 5 minutes over low heat. Uncover and sprinkle additional parsley on top. Squeeze lemon over paella and serve with lemon wedges.

Seared Mushroom Medley

Sautéing mushrooms over a hot stove can be time consuming. In this recipe, mushrooms are placed in a searing hot skillet and later browned in the oven. You can use any combination of mushrooms to create variety. When cleaning mushrooms, simply wipe with a damp paper towel. Do not rinse under the faucet or mushrooms will absorb too much water.

Yield: 6-8 servings | Prep Time: 15 minutes | Cooking Time: 15 minutes
Nutritional Info: Calories: 73, Sodium: 28 mg, Dietary Fiber: 1.5 g, Total Fat: 5.0 g, Total Carbs: 5.5 g, Protein: 3.9 g.

Ingredients:

2 pounds assorted mushrooms, such as white button, cremini, baby Portobello, oyster and shitake
1 yellow onion sliced thin
2 tablespoons butter
1 tablespoon olive oil
2 garlic cloves, minced
2 green onions, sliced thin

Instructions:

1. Preheat oven to 475 degrees. Place cast iron skillet on middle rack in oven to heat for about 15 minutes.

2. Clean mushrooms with damp towel. Slice the mushrooms into mid-sized pieces. Remove pan from oven and place mushrooms in hot pan. Allow mushrooms to sear in hot pan for 5-8 minutes. Remove skillet and turn over mushrooms so that flip side browns.

3. Once mushrooms are seared, add onion, butter and olive oil. Return to oven for 5-7 minutes. Toss in garlic and return pan to oven for another minute. Remove sizzling skillet and garnish with sliced scallions.

Seasoned Beer Battered Onion Rings

Beer is often used in the batter of fried foods because it adds three important elements: carbon dioxide, foaming agents and alcohol- all of which play a role in producing a light, crispy flavorful crust. You can use any type of onion in this recipe, but sweet Vidalia onions are a nice complement to the rich, salty crust of the onion ring. You can also use these onion rings as a topping for the Green Bean Casserole.

Yield: 4 servings | Prep Time: 3 hours | Cooking Time: 20 minutes
Nutritional Info: Calories: 336, Sodium: 538 mg, Dietary Fiber: 4.1 g, Total Fat: 1.3 g, Total Carbs: 64.0 g, Protein: 5.3 g.

Ingredients:

3 large Vidalia onions, sliced into ½ round slices
1 cup buttermilk
Canola oil
2 cups flour
1 tablespoon seasoning blend (such as poultry, steak or Cajun seasoning)
2 cups light beer, any variety
1 teaspoon baking soda
Coarse salt

Instructions:

1. Soak onion rings in buttermilk for 2-3 hours.
2. Heat a large cast iron skillet over medium to high heat.
3. Pour in enough oil to come up to 1 inch in the skillet.
4. Combine flour, seasoning, beer and baking soda in a bowl and mix well.
5. Remove onions from buttermilk mixture and place into flour to coat. Place onion rings into hot pan one at a time. Do not overcrowd pan.
6. Cook until golden brown, turning once, for about 5-6 minutes in total.
7. Place in a single layer on a paper towel to absorb excess oil and sprinkle with salt.

Skillet Mac n' Cheese

Macaroni and cheese made inside a skillet develops beautiful, crusty edges. Traditionally, flour is used to thicken the cheese sauce, but you do not need to use the entire amount. Stop adding flour once the sauce appears thickened but still pourable. Watch the dish carefully in the oven. The panko topping tends to brown quickly.

Yield: 4-6 servings | Prep Time: 15 minutes | Cooking Time: 20 minutes
Nutritional Info: Calories: 470, Sodium: 524 mg, Dietary Fiber: 2.4 g, Total Fat: 19.8 g, Total Carbs: 52.4 g, Protein: 21.5 g.

Ingredients:

12 ounce box rotini or elbow pasta
1 tablespoon butter
1 cup whole or 1% milk
½ teaspoon paprika
¼ teaspoon garlic powder
½ teaspoon salt
¼ teaspoon pepper
2 ½ cups grated cheddar and mozzarella cheese
3-4 tablespoons all-purpose flour
½ cup panko crumbs
1 teaspoon parsley, chopped

Instructions:

1. Preheat oven to 400 degrees.
2. Bring a pot of salted water to a boil. Meanwhile, heat a cast iron skillet over medium heat.
3. Place pasta in boiling water and cook according to package directions.
4. Place butter in hot skillet. Pour in milk, paprika, garlic powder, salt and pepper. Whisk together. Add half the cheese to the skillet slowly, whisking frequently. When it is melted, add flour gradually, whisking constantly to thicken.
5. Drain pasta and add to the skillet. Pour in cheese sauce and stir until pasta is coated. Sprinkle top with other half of cheese and panko crumbs. Transfer to oven and bake 10-15 minutes or until browned. Top with chopped parsley.

Skillet Whole Wheat Flour Tortillas

These easy to make tortillas are far superior to the packaged variety. Not only do they taste fresher, but they are free from the preservatives that processed breads contain. These tortillas are a perfect accompaniment to the Flank Steak Fajita or Mexican Brown Rice Bake recipes in this recipe book. Refrain from rolling out the dough multiple times or it will become tough.

Yield: 12 servings | Prep Time: 40 minutes | Cooking Time: 3 minutes
Nutritional Info: Calories: 175, Sodium: 149 mg, Dietary Fiber: 0.7 g, Total Fat: 9.3 g, Total Carbs: 20.1 g, Protein: 2.7 g.

Ingredients:

2 ½ cups whole wheat flour
¾ teaspoon salt
1 teaspoon baking powder
½ cup vegetable oil
¾ to 1 cup warm water

Instructions:

1. Combine flour, salt and baking powder in a large bowl. Add oil and mix with your fingers.
2. Add the liquid slowly, mixing in enough liquid until a sticky dough forms. You might not need all the liquid.
3. Let rest for about 30 minutes. Divide dough into 12 balls (for medium sized tortillas). Cover with a damp cloth.
4. On a floured surface, roll out each ball into a circle, about ¼ inch thick. Heat a heavy skillet over high heat with a tablespoon of oil and cook the tortilla for 30 seconds on each side. When tortilla looks slightly browned and textured, they are done; do not overcook. Wrap in a damp towel while you cook the others.

Southwest Style Vegetable and Rice Skillet

In this one-skillet meal, the rice cooks right along with the vegetables in the skillet. It is best to use a skillet with a lid in this recipe so that the rice can properly cook; without a lid, too much liquid might evaporate and leave you with undercooked rice. Do not substitute brown rice without adjusting liquid amounts.

Yield: 6-8 servings | Cooking Time: 45 minutes
Nutritional Info: Calories: 265, Sodium: 635 mg, Dietary Fiber: 6.2, Total Fat: 10.5 g, Total Carbs: 36.5 g, Protein: 7.6 g.

Ingredients:

2 tablespoons olive oil
1 yellow onion, sliced
2 plum tomatoes, cut into chunks
2 peppers, green and red, sliced
1 jalapeno pepper, seeded and diced
Salt and pepper
1 cup long grain white rice
1 cup store-bought medium heat salsa
1 (15 ounce can) black beans
1 teaspoon cumin
1 tablespoon chili powder
1 ¾ cup vegetable broth
1 cup shredded Mexican cheese
4 green onions, sliced
1 avocado, diced

Instructions:

1. Heat a cast iron skillet over medium heat and add oil. Sauté onion until softened and showing color, 4-5 minutes. Add tomatoes, peppers, jalapeno, salt and pepper. Stir for several minutes.

2. Add rice, salsa, beans, cumin, chili powder and broth and stir until evenly combined.

111

3. Place a tight lid on skillet, turn up heat and bring to a boil. After it comes to a boil, turn down the heat and simmer for 30-35 minutes. After 35 minutes, remove the lid and check that the rice is fully cooked and tender. Pour cheese on top and let sit on burner until cheese is melted. Turn off the heat. Sprinkle green onions and avocado on top and serve.

Spaghetti Pie

Spaghetti pie is a recipe your kids will love. You will love that you don't need to use separate pots for spaghetti and sauce – the spaghetti cooks inside the skillet and dinner is ready in minutes! You can use a jarred tomato sauce but the sauce in this recipe is simple and adaptable, and adds extra freshness.

Yield: 6 servings | Prep Time: 15 minutes | Cooking Time: 30 minutes
Nutritional Info: Calories: 482, Sodium: 1334 mg, Dietary Fiber: 4.5 g, Total Fat: 25.9 g, Total Carbs: 33.9 g, Protein: 27.8 g.

Ingredients:

1 pound sausage, any variety
3 garlic cloves, minced
28 ounce can crushed tomatoes
½ cup onion, finely diced
½ teaspoon sugar
1 teaspoon Italian seasoning
1 teaspoon salt
¼ teaspoon black pepper
2 cups water
8 ounces linguine
1 cup shredded mozzarella cheese
1 cup chopped basil

Instructions:

1. Preheat oven to 400 degrees.
2. Heat cast iron skillet over medium heat. Add olive oil. Add sausage and garlic, breaking up sausage into pieces. Brown sausage and transfer to a plate.
3. Wipe out skillet and add tomatoes, onion, sugar, seasoning, salt and pepper. Sauté several minutes. Add water and spaghetti noodles and make sure sauce covers the noodles.
4. Bring to a boil and cook 9-12 minutes. Add in sausage and stir. Sprinkle cheese on top and bake in oven for 12-15 minutes or until cheese is bubbly.
5. Remove from oven and top with basil.

Stir-Fried Eggplant with Harissa, Basil and Yogurt

Eggplant is a wonderful vegetable for stovetop cooking as it tends to soften quickly and absorb excess oil in the oven where you cannot watch it closely. Choose small eggplants since they tend to have better flavor. Adding a dollop of yogurt provides a cooling element to this otherwise spicy dish.

Yield: 6 servings | Prep Time: 5 minutes | Cooking Time: 3 minutes
Nutritional Info: Calories: 107, Sodium: 27 mg, Dietary Fiber: 4.0 g, Total Fat: 7.6 g, Total Carbs: 8.8 g, Protein: 2.4 g.

Ingredients:

3 tablespoons olive oil
1 ½ pounds, young, firm eggplant, cut into cubes
Salt and pepper
2 cloves, garlic, sliced
½ - 1 teaspoon harissa
½ cup basil chopped
½ cup plain yogurt

Instructions:

1. Heat cast iron skillet over medium heat. Add 2 tablespoons olive oil and eggplant and stir to coat. Allow eggplant to begin to char. Season with salt and pepper. Cook eggplant a few minutes and remove from skillet.

2. Add remaining tablespoon olive oil and garlic. Cook 1 minute. Add harissa and eggplant to skillet and stir for 1 minute.

3. Remove to plate and top with fresh basil and yogurt. Add more salt if necessary.

Sweet Butternut Squash Cubes

Butternut squash is so versatile; it can be sweet or savory, roasted or pureed. When cubing the squash, try to make uniform cuts so squash cooks evenly. Keep cubes small so that the edges do not burn before squash is fully cooked.

Yield: 4 servings | Prep Time: 2 minutes | Cooking Time: 5 minutes
Nutritional Info: Calories: 154, Sodium: 2 mg, Dietary Fiber: 2.3 g, Total Fat: 14.6 g, Total Carbs: 7.3 g, Protein: 0.8 g.

Ingredients:

2 tablespoons canola oil
4 sage leaves, sliced thinly
1 medium butternut squash, peeled and cut into ½ - ¾ inch cubes
Coarse salt and pepper
2 tablespoons good quality balsamic vinegar
2 tablespoons extra-virgin olive oil
½ teaspoon honey

Instructions:

1. Heat skillet over medium-low heat. Add sage and fry for 30 seconds. Transfer to a plate. Add squash and toss so oil evenly coats the squash. Spread squash in a single layer and stir after a few minutes, making sure not to burn the bottom sides.

2. Lower heat slightly and continue cooking until squash softens. A few pieces may darken more quickly than the others but that is ok.

3. Stir together vinegar, olive oil and honey in a bowl. Remove squash from pan and drizzle with vinegar mixture. Sprinkle with salt and pepper.

Sweet Potato and Black Bean Enchiladas

This vegetarian enchilada recipe calls for cubed sweet potatoes but you can use any starchy, hearty vegetable to take the place of meat or chicken. If you love Mexican flavor but are watching your calories, this enchilada recipe is the perfect meal.

Yield: 4-6 servings | Prep Time: 15 minutes | Cooking Time: 20 minutes
Nutritional Info: Calories: 707, Sodium: 377 mg, Dietary Fiber: 35.9, Total Fat: 12.7 g, Total Carbs: 133.6 g, Protein: 31.9 g.

Ingredients:

2 teaspoons olive oil
2 shallots, diced
2 green onions, sliced thin
3 cloves garlic, minced
3 cups sweet potatoes, cut into ½ inch pieces
½ teaspoon salt
1 teaspoon cumin
1 teaspoon chili powder
½ teaspoon coriander
¼ teaspoon cayenne pepper
¼ teaspoon cinnamon
1 (15 ounce) can black beans, rinsed and drained
½ cup frozen corn, defrosted
8-10 corn tortillas, cut into wedges
1 (15 ounce) can enchilada sauce
1 cup sharp cheddar cheese
2 tablespoons chopped cilantro

Instructions:

1. Preheat oven to 400 degrees.
2. Heat cast iron skillet over medium heat. Add oil, shallots, green onions and garlic and sauté until softened. Add sweet potatoes, salt, cumin, chili powder, coriander, cayenne pepper and cinnamon and cook until sweet potatoes soften, about 10-12 minutes.
3. Pour in the black beans and corn. Layer the tortilla wedges in the skillet. Top with sauce and cheese. Simmer for several minutes and then place in oven until cheese melts. Top with cilantro.

Three-Cheese Penne

Think of this recipe as grown up mac n' cheese. The addition of goat cheese and mascarpone, an Italian cheese made from cream and other acidic elements, provides a wonderful creaminess and sharpness. Be aware that the mascarpone can tend to leave a bit of extra oil in the skillet.

Yield: 6 servings | Prep Time: 15 minutes | Cooking Time: 40 minutes
Nutritional Info: Calories: 586, Sodium: 481 mg, Dietary Fiber: 0.8, Total Fat: 31.0 g, Total Carbs: 50.7 g, Protein: 25.9 g.

Ingredients:

1 pound penne pasta
6 tablespoons unsalted butter
1 small onion, diced
1 garlic clove, crushed
¼ cup flour
1 ½ cups whole milk
1/3 cup mascarpone cheese
1/3 cup goat cheese
8 ounces gruyere cheese, grated
½ teaspoon salt

¼ teaspoon pepper
Chopped fresh parsley

Instructions:

1. Preheat oven to 375 degrees.
2. Place a pot of boiling salted water on high heat and cook pasta according to package directions.
3. Heat cast iron skillet over medium heat. Melt butter and add onion and garlic, cooking until soft, 2-3 minutes.
4. Add flour to skillet and stir constantly for 3 minutes. Pour in milk and continue stirring. Add in mascarpone, goat cheese and 4 ounces gruyere cheese. Stir until thick, about 5 minutes.
5. Season with salt and pepper and add pasta to skillet. Sprinkle remaining 4 ounces gruyere cheese on top and place skillet in oven for 30 minutes, or until bubbly. Sprinkle with parsley.

Tomato, Kale and White Bean Skillet

This one-skillet meal is a great alternative to meat or chicken. The crouton topping adds texture to the creaminess of the beans. If you do not like kale, feel free to use spinach or another leafy green vegetable, such as collard greens.

Yield: 6 servings | Prep Time: 15 minutes | Cooking Time: 40 minutes
Nutritional Info: Calories: 262, Sodium: 933 mg, Dietary Fiber: 8.4, Total Fat: 8.0 g, Total Carbs: 39.2 g, Protein: 11.6 g.

Ingredients:

2 tablespoons extra virgin olive oil
1 tablespoon butter
3 cups day old bread, diced
2 pounds tomatoes, diced

117

2 sprigs thyme
4 garlic cloves, minced
3 shallots, minced
2 teaspoons kosher salt
Pinch of red pepper flakes
1 bunch kale, washed, tough stems discarded and chopped
1 can white beans, drained and rinsed
1 bunch parsley, chopped

Instructions:

1. Preheat oven to 350 degrees.

2. Heat skillet over medium heat. Add oil, butter and bread and stir to coat. Brown bread in skillet for several minutes. Transfer to a dish.

3. Add tomatoes, thyme, garlic, shallots, salt and red pepper flakes. Cook until tomatoes begin to release their juices, about 5 minutes. Add kale and heat until wilted.

4. Take skillet off heat and add white beans and parsley. Sprinkle with sea salt and drizzle with a small amount of extra virgin olive oil. Return croutons to skillet.

5. Bake for 30 minutes or until crouton topping is browned.

Vegetarian Stir-Fry

Making stir-fries is a great way to utilize a cast iron skillet; it retains heat well enough to be a dependable substitute for a wok. But if you are planning on cooking a noodle stir fry, your best bet is to use a non-stick skillet. Even in a well-seasoned pan, noodles tend to stick and make clean up difficult.

Yield: 4 servings | Prep Time: 3 minutes | Cooking Time: 5 minutes
Nutritional Info: Calories: 109, Sodium: 457 mg, Dietary Fiber: 1.7, Total Fat: 7.7 g, Total Carbs: 8.9 g, Protein: 2.3 g.

Ingredients:

2 tablespoons vegetable oil
3 cloves garlic, chopped
1 piece ginger, peeled and diced
2 shallots, thinly sliced
1 cup mixed mushrooms, such as shitake, cremini and Portobello, sliced
1 red bell pepper, cut into thin slices
1 yellow pepper, cut into thin slices
2 tablespoons soy sauce
½ teaspoon toasted sesame oil
2 scallions, diced
Basil leaves, shredded

Instructions:

1. Preheat cast iron skillet over medium heat. Pour oil in skillet. Add garlic and ginger and sauté for one minute. Add shallots and sauté for another 2 minutes, until they color.
2. Add mushrooms and peppers and stir frequently until they soften. Pour in soy sauce and sesame oil and sauté 1 more minute.
3. Transfer to a plate and top with diced scallions and basil leaves.

Veggie Pan Pizza

If you own a large cast iron skillet (10 inches or larger), you will never need to use a pizza stone again. The advantage of a skillet is that the crust will get browned and crispy. Purchasing pre-made pizza dough means you can have this meal on the table in minutes, and the addition of loads of veggies makes it a healthy choice.

Yield: 4 servings | Prep Time: 15 minutes | Cooking Time: 45 minutes
Nutritional Info: Calories: 342, Sodium: 626 mg, Dietary Fiber: 2.5 g, Total Fat: 22.8 g, Total Carbs: 20.3 g, Protein: 15.9 g.

Ingredients:

2 tablespoons olive oil
6 ounces shredded mozzarella cheese
3 tablespoons grated parmesan cheese
½ teaspoon garlic powder
½ teaspoon onion powder
½ box white button mushrooms sliced
1 sweet onion, thinly sliced
2 peppers, any color, sliced
1 head broccoli, broken into small florets
¾ cup prepared tomato or pizza sauce
1 package pizza dough, thawed if necessary
Several large basil leaves

Instructions:

1. Grease a cast iron skillet over medium heat. Preheat oven to 450 degrees.
2. Place mushrooms, onions, peppers and broccoli on a baking sheet with a drizzle of olive oil and salt.
3. Roast veggies for 15-20 minutes.
4. In a mixing bowl, combine cheeses and spices.
5. Spread dough inside skillet. Pour sauce and spread over dough. Add   Ingredients in 3 layers: first cheese mixture, then roasted vegetables, then remaining cheese. On center oven rack, bake pizza for 20-25 minutes or until cheese bubbles. After removing pizza, sprinkle with fresh basil.

Golden Hash Brown Cake

Skillet hash browns makes for a beautiful presentation. This recipe works equally well with sweet potatoes, yams, beets, parsnips or most other root vegetables. Use a box grater or the grating disk on a food processor to shred the potatoes.

Yield: 6-8 servings | Prep Time: 2 minutes | Cooking Time: 20 minutes
Nutritional Info: Calories: 201, Sodium: 591 mg, Dietary Fiber: 3.9 g, Total Fat: 10.4 g, Total Carbs: 25.2 g, Protein: 2.7 g.

Ingredients:

6 russet potatoes, peeled and coarsely grated
2 teaspoons kosher salt
¼ teaspoon fresh black pepper
6 tablespoons vegetable oil

Instructions:

1. Rinse potatoes in a colander and squeeze out excess moisture. Transfer to a bowl and season with salt and pepper.
2. Heat a cast iron skillet over medium heat. Add the oil and allow to smoke. Add potatoes and press down firmly with a spatula. Cook until sides and bottom are golden brown, about 15 minutes.
3. Once cooled, flip skillet onto a plate and invert hash browns. Place back in the skillet with a drop of oil and cook until reverse side browns nicely. Top with additional sea salt.

Sweets and Desserts

"Dessert is probably the most important stage of the meal, since it will be the last thing your guests remember before they pass out all over the table."

William Powell

Apple-Cinnamon Skillet Cake

Baking a cake need not take hours. This delicious, moist cake makes a beautiful presentation with rows of sliced apples in concentric circles on top. Don't skip the step calling for fanning the apples on top after 15 minutes of baking; if you add them into the liquid batter, they will simply sink in.

Yield: 6-8 servings | Prep Time: 15 minutes | Cooking Time: 50 minutes
Nutritional Info: Calories: 228, Sodium: 293 mg, Dietary Fiber: 1.5 g, Total Fat: 7.5 g, Total Carbs: 38.0 g, Protein: 3.9 g.

Ingredients:

1 cup all-purpose flour
½ teaspoon baking powder
½ teaspoon baking soda
½ teaspoon salt
4 tablespoons unsalted butter, room temperature
¾ cup granulated sugar
2 large eggs
½ cup milk
2 apples, any variety, peeled, cored and sliced
Cinnamon- sugar mixture (5 tablespoons sugar, mixed with 1 ½ teaspoons cinnamon)

Instructions:

1. Preheat oven to 350 degrees.
2. Grease a cast iron skillet with butter or cooking spray.
3. Whisk together flour, baking powder, baking soda and salt. In a separate bowl, beat butter and sugar at medium speed with a hand mixer. Beat in eggs. Add flour mixture and milk in several additions, alternating with each addition.
4. Pour batter into skillet. Bake for 15 minutes and remove from oven. Fan apples over batter with cinnamon sugar mixture on top. Bake until top is set and golden brown, another 30 minutes.

123

Banana-Pecan Clafouti

Here is another version of this simple and versatile recipe. The preparation is similar to making waffles or pancakes, but it looks like an elegant dessert that could be served at a fine dining restaurant. This recipe incorporates bananas and pecans for a Southern twist on a French favorite.

Yield: 8 servings | Prep Time: 15 minutes | Cooking Time: 45 minutes
Nutritional Info: Calories: 194, Sodium: 131 mg, Dietary Fiber: 1.1 g, Total Fat: 8.2 g, Total Carbs: 27.2 g, Protein: 4.5 g.

Ingredients:

1 cup whole milk
¼ cup whipping cream
3 eggs
½ cup granulated sugar
1 teaspoon vanilla extract
2 tablespoons butter, melted
¼ teaspoon salt
½ cup all-purpose flour
2 bananas, peeled and thinly sliced
2 teaspoons fresh lemon juice
½ cup pecans, roughly chopped

Instructions:

1. Preheat the oven to 350 degrees.
2. Whisk together milk, cream, eggs, sugar, extract, butter and salt. Add the flour and whisk gently until incorporated.
3. Place sliced bananas in a bowl with lemon juice.
4. Lightly grease a cast iron skillet and heat in oven for 5 minutes. Remove skillet and pour in batter. Scatter bananas and pecans over batter and place in oven. Bake until golden and puffed, about 35 minutes.

Blueberry Slump

A "slump" is a skillet dessert similar to a cobbler. It combines syrupy, warmed fruit with a fluffy dough topping. Substitute any fruit for the blueberries, if you wish. Cook this traditional favorite over an open grill to free up oven space if you are busy baking other items.

Yield: 8 servings | Prep Time: 15 minutes | Cooking Time: 30 minutes
Nutritional Info: Calories: 188, Sodium: 271 mg, Dietary Fiber: 3.2 g, Total Fat: 3.5 g, Total Carbs: 38.5 g, Protein: 3.0 g.

Ingredients:

2 pounds fresh blueberries
1/3 cup sugar
2 tablespoons water
1 ½ tablespoons fresh lime juice
1 cup all-purpose flour
1 teaspoon baking powder
1 teaspoon baking soda
¼ teaspoon kosher salt
½ cup buttermilk
2 tablespoons unsalted butter, melted
1 teaspoon turbinado sugar

Instructions:

1. If cooking indoors, preheat oven to 375 degrees.
2. Preheat cast iron skillet over medium heat. Cook blueberries, sugar, water and lime juice for 10-15 minutes, or until fruit breaks down and thickens.
3. In a separate bowl, whisk together flour, baking powder, baking soda, salt and an additional 1 ½ tablespoons sugar. Add buttermilk and melted butter and stir until a moist dough forms.
4. Scoop dough evenly over fruit mixture in skillet. Sprinkle turbinado sugar on top. Bake in oven or on top of grill for 20-25 minutes until dough sets.

Bourbon Pecan Pie

This pecan pie eliminates the typical corn syrup filing that can make pecan pie look syrupy and clumpy. Make sure your skillet is well seasoned when making recipes with delicate pie crust as they will stick if not properly seasoned. Add extra bourbon for a more distinctive alcohol flavor.

Yield: 8 servings | Prep Time: 20 minutes | Cooking Time: 2 hours and 30 minutes
Nutritional Info: Calories: 346, Sodium: 137 mg, Dietary Fiber: 0.6 g, Total Fat: 18.9 g, Total Carbs: 42.6 g, Protein: 4.1 g.

Ingredients:

½ package refrigerated pie crust
1 tablespoon brown sugar
4 large eggs
1 ½ cups white sugar
½ cup melted butter
½ cup chopped toasted pecans
2 tablespoons all-purpose flour
1 tablespoon cream
1 ½ teaspoons bourbon
½ teaspoon vanilla extract
2 cups pecan halves

Instructions:

1. Preheat oven to 350 degrees.
2. Form pie crust to fit a 10 inch greased cast iron skillet. Sprinkle with brown sugar. Pierce crust and bake for 10 minutes until golden brown.
3. Whisk eggs, white sugar, melted butter, chopped pecans, flour, cream, bourbon and vanilla extract in a large bowl. Pour into pie crust and top with pecan halves, arranged in concentric circles.
4. Transfer skillet to the oven and bake for 25-30 minutes. Turn oven off and let pie stand in oven with door closed for 2 hours.

Deep-Dish Giant Double Chocolate Chip Cookie

This dessert is everyone's favorite – a soft, warm, gooey chocolate chip cookie. The entire recipe can be prepared using just your skillet! Best of all, when you have guests, you can have the batter ready and pour it into the skillet during dinner and take it out at dessert time for a freshly baked dessert that will impress.

Yield: 6-8 servings | Prep Time: 15 minutes | Cooking Time: 30 minutes
Nutritional Info: Calories: 417, Sodium: 299 mg, Dietary Fiber: 1.4 g, Total Fat: 21.1 g, Total Carbs: 53.2 g, Protein: 4.9 g.

Ingredients:

½ cup unsalted butter
½ cup light brown sugar
½ cup white sugar
1 teaspoon vanilla
1 large egg
1 cup all-purpose flour
½ teaspoon baking powder
½ teaspoon salt
1 cup chocolate chip
½ cup chocolate chunks

Instructions:

1. Preheat oven to 350 degrees.
2. Preheat a 10 inch skillet. Melt butter over low heat.
3. Add sugars and stir well. Incorporate vanilla and egg, and beat quickly to make sure eggs do not cook. Stir in flour, baking soda and salt. Fold in chocolate chips and chunks and spread dough out in skillet lightly with a spatula to flatten.
4. Bake for 25 minutes until cookie appears browned on top.

Grilled Fruit Medley

Grilled fruit is a wonderful, healthy alternative to baked desserts. A cast iron pan brings out the sweetness in grilled fruit by caramelizing the exterior. Use a variety of brightly colored fruits for a beautiful presentation.

Yield: 4-6 servings | Prep Time: 5 minutes | Cooking Time: 5 minutes
Nutritional Info: Calories: 169, Sodium: 83 mg, Dietary Fiber: 3.8 g, Total Fat: 1.2 g, Total Carbs: 41.9 g, Protein: 2.7 g.

Ingredients:

Cooking spray
2 tablespoons avocado oil
1 ½ tablespoon sugar
¼ teaspoon sea salt
2 large peaches or nectarines, cut into wedges
5 thick slices watermelon, with rind removed
3 thick slices pineapple, cut into sticks
2 teaspoons fresh lime juice
2 tablespoons chopped mint
1 cup blueberries

Instructions:

1. Heat a cast iron skillet over medium high heat. Spray with cooking spray. Dab a small amount of oil onto fruit. Sprinkle on sugar and sea salt.
2. Place peach wedges, watermelon and pineapple into skillet, working in batches. Cook for 1-2 minutes on each side, until slightly charred and softened.
3. Place fruit on a platter and sprinkle with lime juice, chopped mint and blueberries.

Nutella Brownies

When baking in a cast iron skillet, keep in mind that because of the heat retention properties of cast iron, the dessert will continue baking for several minutes after being removed from the oven. Thus, even if you prefer a cake like consistency to a fudgy texture, do not bake for much longer than the recipe indicates.

Yield: 8 servings | Prep Time: 15 minutes | Cooking Time: 50 minutes
Nutritional Info: Calories: 429, Sodium: 271 mg, Dietary Fiber: 2.4 g, Total Fat: 19.8 g, Total Carbs: 58.4 g, Protein: 6.3 g.

Ingredients:

1 cup sugar
3 large eggs
1 cup all-purpose flour
½ cup Dutch cocoa powder
½ teaspoon salt
½ teaspoon vanilla extract
½ stick unsalted butter
¼ cup half and half
4 ounces chocolate chips
½ cup Nutella spread

Instructions:

1. Preheat oven to 350 degrees.
2. Whisk together sugar and eggs in one bowl. Whisk together flour, cocoa and salt in another bowl.
3. In a cast iron skillet, simmer butter and half and half together over low heat. Add chocolate chips and stir until melted, about 2 minutes. Add in Nutella and continue stirring until incorporated. Remove from heat.
4. Pour sugar mixture into chocolate mixture in skillet. Carefully add flour mixture and fold until just incorporated.
5. Bake for 25 minutes, but start checking at 20 minutes. At about 20-22 minutes, you will have a brownie with a fudge like consistency.

Oatmeal Cherry and Pecan Skillet Cookie

Customize this cookie to suit your family's tastes. Walnuts, dried fruits or shredded coconut are delicious additions. If you want a more rustic looking cookie, use old fashioned rolled oats. For a more uniform texture, use quick cooking oats, which are just coarsely chopped regular oats.

Yield: 8 servings | Prep Time: 15 minutes | Cooking Time: 25 minutes
Nutritional Info: Calories: 293, Sodium: 176 mg, Dietary Fiber: 1.4 g, Total Fat: 14.0 g, Total Carbs: 39.2 g, Protein: 3.7 g.

Ingredients:

½ cup unsalted butter
1 cup brown sugar
1 egg
½ teaspoon baking soda
Pinch of salt
1 teaspoon cinnamon
¼ teaspoon nutmeg
1 ¼ cups all-purpose flour
½ cup quick cooking oatmeal
½ cup toasted pecans, chopped
1 cup dried cherries, chopped in half

Instructions:

1. Preheat oven to 375 degrees.
2. Heat a cast iron skillet over medium heat. Melt butter for several minutes until it foams. Stir in brown sugar. Remove from heat for several minutes.
3. Add egg, baking soda, salt, cinnamon, and nutmeg to the skillet and whisk with sugar. Add flour and stir until just incorporated.
4. Add oatmeal, pecans and cherries and combine well. Pat cookie dough in the skillet to flatten.
5. Bake for 15-18 minutes or until set.

Peach Cobbler

Make your own dough for this peach cobbler. The key is to keep the butter very cold until just before using it. Prebake the crust in the oven to maintain its crispiness. Make sure your peaches are not overripe. You want them to hold their shape after slicing.

Yield: 8 servings | Prep Time: 15 minutes | Cooking Time: 1 hour
Nutritional Info: Calories: 328, Sodium: 146 mg, Dietary Fiber: 2.6 g, Total Fat: 12.0 g, Total Carbs: 53.5 g, Protein: 3.9 g.

Ingredients:

1 ½ cups all-purpose flour
1 teaspoon sugar
¼ teaspoon fine sea salt
1 stick cold butter, cut into pieces
5 to 6 tablespoons cold water
¼ cup all-purpose flour
1 cup light brown sugar
½ lemon, juiced
4 ½ cups peaches, sliced into thin wedges
3 tablespoons sugar
1 tablespoon cinnamon

Instructions:

1. Preheat oven to 375 degrees.
2. To make the crust, mix flour, sugar and salt. Cut in butter with your fingertips. Add water, one tablespoon at a time until mixture is moist. Only pour enough water to make sure dough sticks together.
3. Place dough on a floured surface and roll out dough to one quarter inch thickness. Place dough in oiled 10 inch cast iron skillet. Pierce dough with fork. Bake for about 8-10 minutes or until browned. Remove from oven.

4. In a separate bowl, combine flour, brown sugar, lemon juice and peaches. Toss to coat thoroughly. Pour into prepared crust. Sprinkle with cinnamon-sugar mixture. Bake 40 minutes or until crust is golden and peaches are bubbly.

Rustic Blackberry Galette

If you crave pie, but don't want the hassle of rolling out crusts and crimping edges, then a galette is the answer. It is free form and rustic- perfect for serving out of a cast iron skillet. This recipe adds mint and basil for freshness and balances the sweetness of the fruit.

Yield: 6 servings | Prep Time: 15 minutes | Cooking Time: 45 minutes
Nutritional Info: Calories: 211, Sodium: 27 mg, Dietary Fiber: 8.3 g, Total Fat: 3.7 g, Total Carbs: 44.5 g, Protein: 3.3 g.

Ingredients:

2 pounds fresh blackberries, rinsed and dried
¾ cup granulated sugar
2 tablespoons fresh lime juice
2 teaspoons chopped fresh basil
1 teaspoon chopped fresh mint
Pinch of salt
¼ teaspoon cinnamon
1 teaspoon vanilla extract
1 package store bought puff pastry, thawed
1 egg white, slightly beaten

Instructions:

1. Preheat oven to 375 degrees. Roll out puff pastry and place in greased cast iron skillet. Allow pastry to hang over the sides slightly.
2. Toss together blackberries, sugar, lime juice, basil, mint, salt, cinnamon and vanilla extract.

3. Spread fruit mixture inside pastry dough in skillet. Fold pastry over the berries to cover edges and about ½ way up. Brush egg white over pastry. Place skillet in oven and bake about 40 minutes, until pastry browns.

Strawberry Rhubarb Upside-Down Cake

Strawberry and rhubarb are a traditional combination usually found in pies and cobblers. Here they are the focus of a beautiful ruby-red upside-down cake. Rhubarb looks like pinkish red celery. While it is a vegetable, when cooked in a dessert it has a tart flavor and serves as a nice complement to sweet fruits such as strawberries.

Yield: 8 servings | Prep Time: 15 minutes | Cooking Time: 30 minutes
Nutritional Info: Calories: 286, Sodium: 85 mg, Dietary Fiber: 1.9 g, Total Fat: 9.7 g, Total Carbs: 47.4 g, Protein: 4.4 g.

Ingredients:

1 cup light brown sugar, divided
1/3 cup unsalted butter, melted
2 cups red rhubarb, chopped in cubes
1 pint fresh strawberries, washed and hulled, cut in half
1 cup whole wheat flour
½ teaspoon baking powder
Pinch of salt
3 eggs
½ cup white sugar
½ teaspoon vanilla extract
¼ teaspoon cinnamon
Chopped mint leaves and whipped cream for garnish

Instructions:

1. Preheat the oven to 350 degrees.

2. Combine ½ cup brown sugar and melted butter and pour in skillet, coating bottom of skillet thoroughly.

3. Arrange strawberries and rhubarb in the skillet, filling all the spaces.

4. Mix flour, baking powder and salt in a bowl. In another bowl, beat eggs and gradually add in white sugar and ½ cup brown sugar. Continue beating until light and fluffy. Add vanilla extract and cinnamon and beat 1 more minute.

5. On low speed, add flour mixture to egg mixture and beat until combined. Spread the batter over the fruit carefully so as not to move the fruit. Make sure batter covers fruit entirely.

6. Bake until the top of cake is set and golden. Remove skillet from the oven and run a knife around the edges. Invert onto a platter and wait a couple of minutes before pulling away skillet. Top with fresh mint and whipped cream.

Sweet Cherry Clafouti

This traditional French country dessert resembles something between a cake and a custard. The batter is thick, but once baked it will puff up like a souffle. Try to serve it immediately as it will deflate if you wait too long after removing it from the oven.

Yield: 8 servings | Prep Time: 15 minutes | Cooking Time: 45 minutes
Nutritional Info: Calories: 326, Sodium: 84 mg, Dietary Fiber: 1.1 g, Total Fat: 6.8 g, Total Carbs: 61.8 g, Protein: 4.5 g.

Ingredients:

1 cup whole milk
¼ cup whipping cream
3 eggs
½ cup granulated sugar
1 teaspoon almond extract
2 tablespoons butter, melted
½ cup all-purpose flour
2 cups cherries, pitted and sliced

Powdered sugar

Instructions:

1. Preheat the oven to 350 degrees.
2. Whisk together milk, cream, eggs, sugar, extract and butter. Add the flour and whisk gently until incorporated.
3. Lightly grease a cast iron skillet and heat in oven for 5 minutes.
4. Remove skillet and pour in batter.
5. Scatter cherries all around batter and place in oven. Bake until golden and puffed, about 35 minutes. Dust with powdered sugar.

Sweet Cornbread Wedges

This version of the classic is slightly sweet and buttery. The addition of buttermilk rather than milk keeps the cornbread moist and crumbly. You can make savory variations adding jalapenos or cheese, but this version takes the place of a morning muffin. Make sure not to overmix the mixture once you add the wet to the dry   Ingredients; doing so will create a dry cornbread.

Yield: 8 servings | Prep Time: 15 minutes | Cooking Time: 20 minutes
Nutritional Info: Calories: 204, Sodium: 375 mg, Dietary Fiber: 0.8 g, Total Fat: 13.4 g, Total Carbs: 17.7 g, Protein: 4.7 g.

Ingredients:

1 stick unsalted butter
1 ½ cups ground yellow cornmeal
½ cup all-purpose flour
1 teaspoon baking powder
½ teaspoon baking soda
3 tablespoons granulated sugar
½ teaspoon salt

2 large eggs
1 ½ cups buttermilk
½ cup frozen corn, thawed

Instructions:

1. Preheat oven to 400 degrees.
2. Melt 5 tablespoons butter in the microwave.
3. Whisk together cornmeal, flour, baking powder, baking soda, sugar and salt.
4. In a separate bowl, beat eggs until light and pale yellow. Whisk in buttermilk. Pour wet mixture into dry mixture and lightly incorporate until no dry streaks remain. Fold in melted butter until just combined. Add corn kernels.
5. Preheat cast iron skillet over low to medium heat. Place remaining 3 tablespoons butter in skillet and melt. Pour batter into the hot skillet and bake in oven until golden brown, about 15 minutes. Cut into wedges.

Three Berry Crumble

Skillet dessert recipes are especially tempting since they emerge from the oven hot and bubbly. The heat of the skillet ensures a perfectly browned, crunchy crust. This crumble calls for blueberries, raspberries and blackberries, but any combination of berries works as well. Frozen berries may be used if fresh are not available.

Yield: 8 servings | Prep Time: 15 minutes | Cooking Time: 1 hour
Nutritional Info: Calories: 387, Sodium: 86 mg, Dietary Fiber: 6.5 g, Total Fat: 15.9 g, Total Carbs: 55.9 g, Protein: 5.7 g.

Ingredients:

6 cups of fresh mixed berries, washed and dried
¼ cup of sugar
¼ cup of flour
1 tablespoon lemon juice

¾ *cup flour*
¾ *cup brown sugar*
¾ *cup old fashioned oats*
½ *cup chopped almonds*
1 teaspoon cinnamon
1 stick cold butter, cut into cubes

Instructions:

1. Preheat oven to 375 degrees.
2. Lightly toss the berries, sugar, flour and lemon juice inside your cast iron skillet.
3. In a bowl, mix the flour, brown sugar, oats, almonds and cinnamon. Incorporate cold butter with your fingertips into the oat mixture until small clumps form.
4. Pour topping onto fruit and bake for 45 minutes to 1 hour, until bubbles form and top appears browned and crispy. Serve with vanilla ice cream right out of the skillet.

Traditional Apple Pie

Making apple pie has never been so simple! Turbinado sugar is light brown sugar cane that comes in the form of large sugar crystals. It looks pretty sprinkled over the top crust and adds some texture to the buttery crust.

Yield: 6-8 servings | Prep Time: 15 minutes | Cooking Time: 1 hour and 5 minutes
Nutritional Info: Calories: 340, Sodium: 90 mg, Dietary Fiber: 5.7 g, Total Fat: 9.9 g, Total Carbs: 67.0 g, Protein: 1.3 g.

Ingredients:

4 pounds apples (such as Braeburn, Granny Smith or Golden delicious), peeled, cored and sliced into ½ inch thick wedges
1 teaspoon ground cinnamon
¼ teaspoon apple pie spice

137

¾ cup granulated sugar
3 teaspoons lemon juice
6 tablespoons butter
¾ cup brown sugar
1 package refrigerated pie crusts
1 egg white
1 ½ tablespoons turbinado sugar

Instructions:

1. Preheat oven to 350 degrees.
2. Toss peeled apples with cinnamon, apple pie spice, sugar and lemon juice in a bowl.
3. Melt butter in a cast iron skillet over low to medium heat and add brown sugar. Cook for 2 minutes until sugar dissolves. Remove heat and spread 1 pie crust in skillet over melted sugar.
4. Pour in apple mixture and spread evenly. Top with remaining piecrust. Whisk egg white and brush piecrust with egg white. Sprinkle top with turbinado sugar. Cut in several slits on top crust.
5. Bake for 45 minutes to 1 hour or until fruit mixture bubbles. Cover with foil if edges began to darken.

Gooey Chocolate Fudge Cake

This chocolate cake is dense, fudgy and best served warm. Use natural cocoa powder to make this cake, not Dutch Processed cocoa. When natural cocoa is used with baking soda, it initiates a leavening process that causes the batter to rise when heated.

Yield: 8 servings | Prep Time: 15 minutes | Cooking Time: 25 minutes
Nutritional Info: Calories: 290, Sodium: 91 mg, Dietary Fiber: 1.0 g, Total Fat: 14.9 g, Total Carbs: 38.5 g, Protein: 2.9 g.

Ingredients:

1 cup flour
½ teaspoon baking soda
1 cup sugar
Pinch of salt
½ cup vegetable oil
3 tablespoons cocoa powder
½ cup water
¼ cup whole milk
1 egg
1 teaspoon vanilla extract

Instructions:

1. Preheat the oven to 350 degrees.
2. In a large bowl, whisk together flour, baking soda, sugar and salt.
3. Combine oil, cocoa powder and water in another bowl. Whisk in flour mixture and pour into skillet.
4. Incorporate milk, egg and vanilla into the batter.
5. Add to skillet and bake for 25 minutes, or until edges are set and center is only slightly jiggly.

Breakfast

"All happiness depends on a leisurely breakfast."
John Gunther

Apple Dutch Baby Pancake

This apple pancake-like soufflé is equally impressive as a dessert. When baking this recipe or any recipe with apples, a tart, crispy variety works best. Try Granny Smith apples for the right balance of sweetness and tartness. The almond extract adds a hint of nuttiness to the sweet, custardy apples.

Yield: 4-6 servings | Prep Time: 15 minutes | Cooking Time: 20 minutes
Nutritional Info: Calories: 240, Sodium: 201 mg, Dietary Fiber: 2.4 g, Total Fat: 11.4 g, Total Carbs: 29.2 g, Protein: 6.0 g.

Ingredients:

3 large eggs, room temperature
¾ cup whole milk
¾ cup all-purpose flour
1 teaspoon almond extract
¼ teaspoon salt
2 large Granny Smith apples, peeled, cored and sliced
1 tablespoon sugar
1 teaspoon cinnamon
½ teaspoon ginger
4 tablespoons butter, divided
2 tablespoons light brown sugar

Instructions:

1. Preheat oven to 400 degrees.
2. Whisk together eggs, milk, flour, extract and salt.
3. Place sliced apples in a bowl with sugar, cinnamon and ginger.
4. Melt 2 tablespoons butter in heated cast iron skillet. Sprinkle brown sugar inside skillet. Add apples and cook until apples have softened. Transfer to plate.
5. Wipe out skillet and melt remaining 2 tablespoons butter. Make sure to coat sides of skillet as well. When skillet is very hot, add apples and pour batter inside skillet. Bake until puffed and golden, about 13-15 minutes.

Bacon and Cheese Frittata

Once you have mastered the basic technique, you can add anything to a frittata. With the addition of meats and vegetables, frittatas go way beyond a breakfast food. They can be a satisfying, well-rounded lunch or dinner. When whisking your eggs, remember to be gentle. Over-beating eggs may result in a flat frittata.

Yield: 8 servings | Prep Time: 15 minutes | Cooking Time: 15 minutes
Nutritional Info: Calories: 255, Sodium: 632 mg, Dietary Fiber: 0 g, Total Fat: 18.8 g, Total Carbs: 1.3 g, Protein: 19.5 g.

Ingredients:

8 slices bacon, chopped
12 large eggs
3 tablespoons milk
Coarse salt
Freshly ground pepper
¼ cup Romano cheese
½ cup grated cheddar cheese
Dash of hot sauce

Instructions:

1. Preheat oven to 375 degrees.
2. Heat cast iron skillet and cook bacon over medium heat, stirring until crisp. Set aside on a plate.
3. In a large bowl, whisk eggs, milk, salt, pepper, cheeses and hot sauce. Add cooked bacon to egg mixture. Pour eggs into cast iron skillet. When eggs are half set and edges begin to pull away, place frittata in oven and bake for about 10 minutes, or until center is no longer jiggly. Cut into wedges inside skillet or slide out of skillet onto serving plate.

Bacon n' Eggs Skillet Breakfast

This is a great recipe for outdoor cooking using your skillet over an open fire. You can cook this dish to resemble more of a hash by scrambling everything together. When doing so, be sure your skillet is well seasoned or that there is sufficient fat in the pan so eggs do not stick to the surface.

Yield: 4 servings | Cooking Time: 15 minutes
Nutritional Info: Calories: 374, Sodium: 631 mg, Dietary Fiber: 4.1 g, Total Fat: 17.3 g, Total Carbs: 31.8 g, Protein: 23.2 g.

Ingredients:

4 strips bacon, chopped
1 small onion, finely chopped
3 medium, potatoes, boiled and cut into cubes
1 tomato, diced
6 eggs, beaten
2 tablespoons milk
Salt and pepper
½ cup mozzarella cheese
Dash hot pepper sauce

Instructions:

1. In a cast iron skillet, fry bacon until crisp, 3-4 minutes. Transfer to a plate. Leave bacon fat in skillet.

2. Add onion and sauté until onion softens, 3-4 minutes. Brown potatoes with onion, another 5 minutes. Add diced tomato. Transfer to plate with bacon.

3. Combine eggs and milk in a bowl and pour into skillet. Season with salt and pepper. Transfer bacon and vegetables into skillet and top with cheese. Let stand on burner until cheese melts. Add a pinch of hot pepper sauce.

Blueberry Buttermilk Pancakes

You can always use a "just add water" pancake mix but homemade pancakes are a great weekend treat. When making pancakes in a cast iron skillet, you can make one large pancake and slice it, almost like a cake, or make individual pancakes. The former will give you nice, browned edges. It is preferable to bring eggs to room temperature when making certain baked goods. Eggs whip up to a greater volume when they have warmed up a bit, therefore producing a fluffier textured pancake.

Yield: 6 servings | Prep Time: 15 minutes | Cooking Time: 30 minutes
Nutritional Info: Calories: 171, Sodium: 477 mg, Dietary Fiber: 1.2 g, Total Fat: 5.2 g, Total Carbs: 27.3 g, Protein: 4.4 g.

Ingredients:

1 cup all-purpose flour
3 tablespoons granulated sugar
1 teaspoon baking powder
1 teaspoon baking soda
Dash of cinnamon
½ teaspoon salt
¾ cup buttermilk
1 large egg, room temperature
2 tablespoons unsalted butter, melted
1 cup blueberries

Instructions:

1. Preheat oven to 375 degrees. Place skillet in oven.
2. Whisk together flour, sugar, baking powder, baking soda, cinnamon and salt.
3. In a separate bowl, whisk together buttermilk, egg and melted butter.
4. Combine the two mixtures until just incorporated.
5. Remove skillet from oven and grease skillet. Pour batter into skillet and top with blueberries. Bake until golden and cooked through, about 25 minutes. Serve with maple syrup.

Cherry Almond Breakfast Scones

Scones are a mildly sweetened biscuit-like cake that are generally dry and slightly dense. Cut into symmetrical wedges for a classic presentation. Any dried fruit, fresh fruit or nut can be substituted for dried cherries and almonds.

Yield: 6-8 servings | Prep Time: 15 minutes | Cooking Time: 25 minutes
Nutritional Info: Calories: 317, Sodium: 97 mg, Dietary Fiber: 4.0 g, Total Fat: 15.3 g, Total Carbs: 40.2 g, Protein: 5.6 g.

Ingredients:

2 cups all-purpose flour
2 teaspoons baking powder
3 tablespoons brown sugar
Pinch of salt
½ cup cold butter
1 ½ cups dried cherries
Zest of one lemon
½ cup chopped almonds
¾ cup milk
½ teaspoon cinnamon
2 tablespoons turbinado sugar

Instructions:

1. Preheat oven to 375 degrees.
2. Combine flour, baking powder, brown sugar and salt. Add cold butter, cut into small pieces, and pinch until dough becomes crumbly.
3. Add dried cherries, zest and chopped almonds to combine. Add the milk and mix dough gently. Do not overwork dough.
4. Grease a cast iron skillet and spread dough uniformly inside the skillet.
5. Combine cinnamon and turbinado sugar and sprinkle on top.
6. Bake for about 25 minutes or until scone is cooked through.

145

Baked Fruit Oatmeal

This oatmeal dish is a great way to prepare breakfast the night before and microwave it in the morning. You can replace water with the milk if you prefer water in your oatmeal. The eggs bind together the oats and fruit to create a big, nutritious oatmeal cookie.

Yield: 4-6 servings | Prep Time: 15 minutes | Cooking Time: 35 minutes
Nutritional Info: Calories: 183, Sodium: 48 mg, Dietary Fiber: 5.0 g, Total Fat: 4.0 g, Total Carbs: 30.4 g, Protein: 7.9 g.

Ingredients:

2 cups old fashioned rolled oats
1 teaspoon baking powder
2 teaspoons brown sugar
½ teaspoon cinnamon
¼ cup unsweetened coconut flakes
2 cups low fat milk
2 egg whites
1 teaspoon vanilla extract
1 cup blueberries
1 cup raspberries

Instructions:

1. Preheat oven to 350 degrees.
2. Combine oats, baking powder, brown sugar, cinnamon and coconut flakes into a greased cast iron skillet.
3. Add milk, egg whites and vanilla and stir well.
4. Add fruits and combine gently so as not to break up fruit.
5. Cook for 30-35 minutes until set and golden brown.

Cinnamon-Sugar French Toast

While French toast is often made with regular old white bread, using French bread for this breakfast treat yields a heartier and more flavorful result. You can adjust the spice mixture, but the addition of nutmeg and ground cloves complements the cinnamon flavor.

Yield: 4 servings | Prep Time: 2 minutes | Cooking Time: 5 minutes
Nutritional Info: Calories: 406, Sodium: 647 mg, Dietary Fiber: 2.3 g, Total Fat: 13.6 g, Total Carbs: 54.8 g, Protein: 17.0 g.

Ingredients:

1 cup whole milk
4 eggs
1 teaspoon cinnamon
1/8 teaspoon nutmeg
1/8 teaspoon ground cloves
2 tablespoons sugar
Pinch of salt
8-10 slices French bread
2 tablespoons unsalted butter

Instructions:

1. Beat together the milk, eggs, cinnamon, nutmeg, cloves, sugar and salt.
2. Heat a cast iron skillet to medium heat.
3. Dredge bread inside egg mixture, turning over several times.
4. Add butter to cast iron skillet and melt until foaming. Lay bread slices inside skillet and cook 2-3 minutes on each side, until browned. Sprinkle with additional cinnamon-sugar or serve with maple syrup.

Easy Dutch Baby Pancake

A Dutch Baby or German pancake is a sweet popover. It deflates quickly after being removed from the oven so serve immediately. Garnish with powdered sugar, maple syrup or fruit toppings.

Yield: 4-6 servings | Prep Time: 15 minutes | Cooking Time: 20 minutes
Nutritional Info: Calories: 138, Sodium: 84 mg, Dietary Fiber: 0 g, Total Fat: 9.0 g, Total Carbs: 9.2 g, Protein: 4.9 g.

Ingredients:

3 large eggs, at room temperature
½ cup all-purpose flour
½ cup whole milk
Dash of salt
¼ teaspoon cinnamon
½ teaspoon vanilla extract
3 tablespoons unsalted butter

Instructions:

1. Preheat oven to 400 degrees.
2. Whisk eggs in a bowl. Add flour, milk, salt, cinnamon and vanilla and whisk until incorporated.
3. Melt butter in a cast iron skillet over medium heat. Add in batter and place skillet in oven for about 15 minutes. Pancake should be puffy and golden brown. Garnish with your favorite topping.

Fluffy Skillet Frittata

This recipe is for a basic frittata, which is similar to a crust-less quiche. The word "frittata" is Italian and means fried. Frittatas are generally begun on the stove and transferred into the oven so the egg cooks through. The addition of milk keeps the frittata light and fluffy.

Yield: 4 servings | Prep Time: 15 minutes | Cooking Time: 15 minutes
Nutritional Info: Calories: 156, Sodium: 147 mg, Dietary Fiber: 0 g, Total Fat: 11.9 g, Total Carbs: 1.0 g, Protein: 11.3 g.

Ingredients:

8 eggs
2 tablespoons whole milk
Coarse salt
Freshly ground pepper
1 tablespoon butter

Instructions:

1. Preheat oven to 400 degrees. Heat a cast iron skillet over medium heat.
2. In a large bowl, whisk eggs, milk, salt and pepper. Pour eggs into cast iron skillet. When eggs are half set and edges begin to pull away, place frittata in the oven and bake for about 10 minutes, or until center is no longer jiggly. Cut into wedges inside skillet or slide out of skillet onto serving plate.

Healthy Pancakes

Feel good about feeding your kids delicious, traditional breakfast foods. These pancakes have a few substitutions that make them healthier than your standard recipe. Whole wheat flour replaces processed white flour and agave is used instead of white sugar. Non-fat milk and egg whites reduce the fat and cholesterol content. Last, the addition of flaxseed provides essential vitamins and minerals, such as iron, zinc and potassium, in addition to omega-3 fatty acids.

Yield: 6 servings | Prep Time: 5 minutes | Cooking Time: 5 minutes
Nutritional Info: Calories: 209, Sodium: 376 mg, Dietary Fiber: 1.2 g, Total Fat: 6.5 g, Total Carbs: 30.9 g, Protein: 6.4 g.

Ingredients:

1 ½ cups whole wheat flour
3 ½ teaspoons baking powder
¾ teaspoon salt

1 tablespoon flax seed
1 tablespoon agave syrup
1 ¼ cups fat-free milk
2 egg whites
3 tablespoons butter, melted
Fresh cut fruit for topping

Instructions:

1. Preheat a cast iron skillet over medium heat. Spray liberally with cooking spray.
2. Combine flour, baking powder, salt and flax seed in a bowl.
3. In another bowl, mix agave, milk, egg whites and melted butter. Pour flour mixture into egg mixture and fold until just incorporated with a rubber spatula.
4. Pour ¼ cup of batter into skillet and brown, 2-3 minutes on each side or until set.
5. Serve with fresh cut fruit.

Middle Eastern Shakshuka

This middle-eastern favorite is a flavorful, filling breakfast and can be easily customized to suit your desired heat level. Remember to remove the seeds of the chili to control the heat. Use canned chopped tomatoes if you do not have fresh tomatoes; they work equally well.

Yield: 2 servings | Prep Time: 5 minutes | Cooking Time: 10 minutes
Nutritional Info: Calories: 225, Sodium: 70 mg, Dietary Fiber: 2.9 g, Total Fat: 19.1 g, Total Carbs: 9.2 g, Protein: 7.3 g.

Ingredients:

2 tablespoons olive oil
½ yellow onion, diced
1 can chopped tomatoes
½ green pepper, diced
1 small serrano or jalapeno chili, seeds removed, diced

1 teaspoon cumin
1 teaspoon paprika
½ teaspoon smoked paprika
¼ teaspoon coriander
2 eggs
Salt and pepper
Chopped parsley or cilantro

Instructions:

1. Preheat a cast iron skillet over medium heat.
2. Heat olive oil in skillet and sauté onion until softened.
3. Add tomatoes, green pepper and chili. Cook for 4-5 minutes. Add seasonings and cook for several minutes until liquid slightly reduces.
4. Make two indentations in mixture and crack eggs into them. Cover and cook until eggs are done. Sprinkle with salt, pepper, parsley and/or cilantro and serve while bubbly and hot.

Sausage and Mushroom Casserole

This casserole, similar to a crust-less quiche, is a great option when you need to feed guests at a brunch. The addition of a Portobello mushrooms adds a heartiness to the dish and substitutes for the traditional potatoes found in breakfast casseroles.

Yield: 6 servings | Prep Time: 15 minutes | Cooking Time: 10 minutes
Nutritional Info: Calories: 275, Sodium: 454 mg, Dietary Fiber: 1.0 g, Total Fat: 20.7 g, Total Carbs: 4.5 g, Protein: 17.6 g.

Ingredients:

½ pound ground sausage, any variety
1 yellow onion, diced
2 large Portobello mushroom caps, wiped clean and cut into chunks

151

Salt and pepper
4 large eggs
2 tablespoons chives
2 spring onions, sliced thin
1 cup cheddar cheese, grated
¼ cup whole milk

Instructions:

1. Preheat oven to 375 degrees.
2. Heat a cast iron skillet over medium heat and sauté sausage for 3-4 minutes. Add onions and continue sauteeing until onion softens. Transfer to a plate.
3. With fat in the pan, add Portobello mushroom pieces and cook until liquid evaporates. Sprinkle with salt and pepper. Set aside.
4. In a mixing bowl, combine eggs, chives, green onion, half of the cheddar cheese and milk. Whisk all the   Ingredients together. Add in sausage, onions and mushrooms.
5. Pour into the greased cast iron skillet and top with remaining half of cheese. Bake for 30 minutes or until cheese melts and bubbles.

Vegan Frittata

If you need a delicious way to use up the veggies in your fridge, whip up this frittata. When you have multiple   Ingredients, the cast iron skillet does double duty: sauteing the fillings and cooking the final product. This is also a great way to get kids to eat green leafy vegetables.

Yield: 8 servings | Prep Time: 15 minutes | Cooking Time: 15 minutes
Nutritional Info: Calories: 177, Sodium: 278 mg, Dietary Fiber: 0 g, Dietary Fiber: 1.6 g, Total Fat: 10.7 g, Total Carbs: 10.0 g, Protein: 11.5 g.

Ingredients:

12 large eggs

3 tablespoons milk
Coarse salt
Freshly ground pepper
2 tablespoons butter
1 medium onion, thinly sliced
1 baked potato, cooled and diced
½ carton mushrooms, cleaned and sliced
2 cups torn spinach leaves, washed
1 small jar sundried tomatoes, chopped

Instructions:

1. Preheat oven to 375 degrees.
2. In a large bowl, whisk eggs, milk, salt and pepper.
3. In a large cast iron skillet, melt butter over medium heat. Add onions and cook several minutes until softened and translucent. Add potatoes and stir with onion. Add mushrooms and cook until slightly colored. Add spinach and sundried tomatoes and stir to incorporate.
4. Pour egg mixture on top of vegetables and make sure   Ingredients are evenly covered. Let frittata sit on burner for 2 minutes and then place in oven.
5. Bake for about 10 minutes, or until center is set. Cut into wedges inside skillet or slices.

Sunny Side-Up Egg and Hash Breakfast

Instead of serving eggs with hash browns on the side, this recipe offers up a complete meal. Purchase frozen shredded potatoes to eliminate the process of shredding and peeling potatoes yourself. Serve alongside a toasted biscuit or bagel.

Yield: 8 servings | Prep Time: 15 minutes | Cooking Time: 25 minutes
Nutritional Info: Calories: 124, Sodium: 77 mg, Dietary Fiber: 1.7 g, Total Fat: 6.7 g, Total Carbs: 10.5 g, Protein: 5.9 g.

Ingredients:

3 cups frozen shredded potatoes
2 tablespoons butter
1 medium onion, diced
1 garlic clove, minced
Salt and pepper
6 large eggs
Sour cream and chives

Instructions:

1. Preheat oven to 350 degrees.
2. Heat skillet over medium heat. Melt butter in cast iron skillet. Add onion and garlic and sauté 4 -5 minutes or until softened. Stir in shredded potatoes and salt and pepper. Sauté until potatoes are cooked and golden in color.
3. Make 6 indentations in the potato mixture. Crack an egg into each indentation and sprinkle with salt and pepper.
4. Bake for 10-12 minutes or until eggs are set.

About The Author

Lisa Brian is a private chef extraordinaire who has prepared meals and specialty foods and beverages for many celebrities along California's coast, from Los Angeles and San Francisco. She has a background in nutrition, and is a highly trained chef. When she's not writing books, she spends her time developing new recipes and cooking up fresh servings of health and happiness for her clients and her family.

Lightning Source UK Ltd.
Milton Keynes UK
UKHW051005170121
377160UK00008B/247